MW01272984

Workplace Evolution

Common Sense for Uncommon Times

Gayle A. Gregory

Pure Possibility, LLC
Hood River, Oregon

Copyright 2009 by Gayle A. Gregory

All rights reserved. No part of this book may be reproduced or
transmitted in any form or by any means, electronic or mechan-
ical, including photocopying, recording or by any information
storage and retrieval systems without permission in writing from
the publisher or author.

Library of Congress Catalog Card Number: 2009929101

ISBN: 978-0-9789191-1-5

Published by Pure Possibility, LLC
2121 Reed Rd., Hood River, Oregon 97031

This book is dedicated to enlightened managers across the world who have seen the seed of potential within individuals and found their own unique ways to coax it to the surface. It is dedicated as well to those of us, who regardless how hard we tried, didn't appear to succeed. Each of us needs someone who believes in us and can see what we are truly capable of, even when, at times, we can not see it ourselves. When a seed is given the time and resources to develop and grow, a tiny shoot of confidence breaks through and changes the course of history.

Table of Contents

Acknowledgments

I could not have written this book without the encouragement of my husband Ken, who understood the significance of the message and was willing to put aside his needs to support me. I can never thank him enough for his love without conditions. My co-founders at Workplace Evolution, Sherri Petro and Vasi Huntalas, have cheered me on, all the while acting as editors and friends, partners and breaths of inspiration. I am indebted and am blessed by each of you.

Through the process of bringing this book into form, I discovered the importance of seasoned guidance. Ursula Bacon was my guiding hand. She took my manuscript and helped me shape difficult concepts into easily readable and understandable ideas. I still marvel at how her questions infused clarity into my work. She has truly been a Godsend. When I read *Shanghai Diary,* her first book, I didn't know that she would grow to be such an important friend and mentor.

I would also like to thank the incredible people whose stories line the pages of this book. Thank you for taking the time to talk with me. You inspired me with the ways you are consciously furthering workplace evolution.

Lastly, I am grateful to my teacher, Elle Collier Re, of Inei-Re and HeartGate Sanctuary. Her precise teachings for the past eleven years shaped my heart and mind, honing the messenger so that I could hear the message and comprehend its potential to enrich us all.

Chapter 1

Evolution – The Nature of Things

In times of change, the learners will inherit the earth while the learned will find themselves beautifully equipped to deal with a world that no longer exists.

— Eric Hoffer

A History of Change

Evolution is happening. How evolution is happening doesn't really matter. Did we evolve from a single cell billions of years ago, or is the world only 6,000 years old? Is evolution an effect of the 100th monkey, a tipping point phenomenon discovered in 1958? What role, if any, did the Big Bang play? Is Darwin's theory of natural selection driving change, or is transformation part of a much larger divine plan? Those are questions for science and religion. This question, "Which evolutionary adaptation is barreling down upon us right now?" is for organizations — non-profits, businesses, government, community clubs — and all other groups of people who come together in a workplace.

No intelligent person questions that change is taking place. All we have to do is look around. Change is a fact of life. According to the former U.S. Secretary of Education, Richard Riley, the top 10

1

in-demand jobs for 2010 did not exist in 2004.[1] Our job choices for the future, beliefs we held, things we thought impossible, have been proven wrong, and if not wrong, proven to be short-sighted. Standing too close to yesterday's news limits perspective. The U.S. auto industry provides a telling example.

"GM sold millions of Cavaliers in the 1980s — and decided the thrifty car was so successful the company didn't need to update it for more than a decade... Honda and Toyota, meanwhile, were updating their competing models every four or five years, and grabbing market share with each quality improvement. A new Cavalier came out in the mid 1990s — then languished for another decade, while GM put most of its money into big trucks and SUVs." [2]

Success limited GM's perspective and their ability to appreciate the bigger picture. They didn't understand that the view is always expanding and that in order to stay in business one can't discount the changes taking place. Our picture gets bigger each day as more information becomes available and if we want our organizations to thrive, it's time to widen our focus.

Evolution is like that. Change is inherent in each moment. If the universe obeyed our pleas to stop changing, our world would actually come to a full stop. Change in that sense would mean the death of everything. From the microcosm to the macro, everything is constant change — evolutionary movement. Evolution is the nature of Nature. If we look at our bodies in a microscope or the heavens in a telescope, we see change.

When we take the time to look at our world, we realize that with each passing day we are seeing countless new pieces of an intricate and constantly expanding[3] mystery. Our universe is expanding, as is consciousness, and with it, our ability to tap into new frontiers of knowledge. Nothing is as simple as it once seemed. Additional dimensions of complexity are emerging. This complexity has always been present. Only now, as we become more aware, and as more pieces come into view, we can see the interconnections and dependencies that previously eluded us.

For many around the world, tears flowed November 4, 2008 when the 44th American president was elected. With their ballots the American public chose inclusion over exclusion, hope over fear. They entered into an era of new possibility, full of optimism and dreams of a brighter future for themselves and their descendants. Cheers resounded coast to coast and around the globe.

We are starting to care for more than just ourselves. This broader focus is a bit more instinctive. Self-focus alone feels empty. The time has come to expose it for the partial answer it is and mark an important point in history. We are recognizing that something vitally important is missing. We know there is another way, different and better, to run our lives and our businesses.

With this new understanding, increasing numbers of us no longer believe we have the right to choose personal gain over the well-being of us all. Enlightened voices across the planet are gaining momentum as they are greeted by a new, interested audience. The Green Movement, one visible facet of this new awareness, is a testament to that fact. No longer an edge concept, it is making inroads into the mainstream, and impacting buying decisions and company bottom lines.

Wall Street's 2008 implosion signaled another shift. Making money at any cost is not excusable, nor is it capable of supporting us long-term individually, organizationally or globally. It isn't now, nor was it during the years leading up to the 1929 Wall Street crash. Unfortunately, we didn't learn our lesson from The Great Depression. In 1932, Ferdinand Pecora, Chief Counsel to the U.S. Senate's Committee on Banking and Currency, took on the financial giants like J.P. Morgan Jr. and Charles Mitchell. Despite the legislation enacted as a result of the hearings, he seemed to understand that his investigation had failed to effect significant change. Words from his memoirs echo loudly with forgotten lessons and lost chances.

"As soon as business recovered the titans of finance developed once again an arrogant self-confidence and a dogmatic assurance that any attempt to restrain their own activities must inevitably mean the ruin of the country."[4]

Those of us who had our homes on the market just before the collapse of 2008 had the chance to learn our own lessons. Even though we knew that housing prices were insane and certain to fall, we hoped to take advantage of the feeding frenzy and get high prices for our properties. If we had opened our eyes for any length of time we would have noticed that soaring prices were damning our children and grandchildren. Unless they inherited the money or struck it rich some other way, they would never feel the joy or know the dignity associated with being able to buy their own home.

My husband and I had our home on the market just before it crashed. We were sitting on a nice five acre plot that was ripe for development — our little nest egg. I remember more than once hoping the boundary changes would be finalized in time for us to sell before the bottom dropped out of the market. We ignored the implications and told ourselves that while it was ridiculous, it was just the way it was. It was uncomfortable, but the misgiving didn't change our asking price. We saw the real estate market as our big chance to ensure our financial security. A belief in lack, that down the road we might not have enough money, was in control. This is just one example of millions in a society run amok. Add them all together and 2008 is easier to understand.

We are painfully and belatedly learning the lessons of careless and indifferent choices, both organizationally and personally. This time though, we have the opportunity to choose a true and lasting makeover, a transformation in fact, rather than change intended to last just until the difficulty passes.

We can stop and look at how the world outside of us is changing and gather insights. We can also observe ourselves and see the ways in which we too, are rigid and inflexible, and learn to reinvent ourselves and adapt to changing times. With inquiry our contribution to and responsibility for the world around us comes into clearer focus. And, if we are willing to accept the possibility that humans are basically alike, we can then be our own best tool to decipher what not only created our current situation, but the best ways to move forward and create something better.

To understand workplace implications we have only to ask ourselves several revealing questions and keep in mind that those around us have similar needs and wants. How do we feel about work? We gain more information when we stop and determine whether our workplaces offer what we ourselves would want from them if we stood in the shoes of our employees, volunteers or other stakeholders. If we were given two equal job offers, what would influence our choice? The decision will likely be driven by what we want from our job and how each offer fits our criteria. Is the potential of being valued and respected a criterion? To see how this works, think about how it feels to be valued and respected, as well as how it feels when we are not. Being esteemed energizes us and makes us want to get out of bed and come to work? Even doing undemanding chores can energize us if we are met with appreciation, and understand the reasoning and importance of the task.

Meaning holds another clue. What is meaningful work? The answer to that question is different for each of us. One man's rubbish is another's treasure. Some of us enjoy repetition, others despise it. Some prefer action, others like introspection. Regardless, with meaning's presence or absence, however we define it, we respond in similar ways. Insert yourself into a picture of life or work without meaning. Sadly, for some of us, this isn't difficult. Many of our workplaces are simply a means to and end, that being a paycheck. Whether the lack of meaning is caused by a CEO or entry-level manager who has all the answers, our own disengagement as a result of waiting to be told what to do next, or any number of other reasons, irrelevance sets performance into slow-motion. Going to work sinks to a low priority and the odds of getting good work done slips even lower. Perhaps a more potent exercise would be to ponder a workplace filled with meaning, purpose and usefulness. The words of Orville Wright, co-inventor of the airplane, capture the sentiment well.

> "Will and I could hardly wait for the morning to come to get at something that interested us. That's happiness."

Community — belonging to something bigger than ourselves — is another key. Does belonging make a difference? Is it significant or unimportant? If we think back to our most effective times, we gain further appreciation by looking at what made us want to do good work, and on the flipside, what disengaged us. When we are truly happy, whether at work or in our personal lives, if we investigate the source of that happiness we can uncover great wisdom. The same can be said of the times when we find ourselves disillusioned and disconnected.

As we ask ourselves these important questions, we can see what positively drives and inspires us, and get a better idea of the importance of meaning, community, and being valued and respected. Our reluctance or willingness to understand this powerful data determines the choices and decisions we make. Either way, we consequentially impact bottom line results. Our choices help us integrate components of a genuinely healthy workplace or breed higher healthcare costs. They set the tone of passionate participation or disengagement and resignation. Our decisions inspire a flow of creativity and innovation or unimaginative repetition. We attract and retain talented people or drain human treasuries. Ultimately, we mold our future and cast our vote for our organization's evolution or eventual extinction.

When we look at our experience to discern what is true, rather than trying to mold the picture to our way of thinking, we see what actually is occurring. Many ideas and values that took hold during the last fifty years set us adrift in individual-sized boats. It was a natural outcome of a me generation. If we couldn't pull ourselves up by our bootstraps we weren't trying hard enough and didn't deserve to succeed. We've all encountered the sentiment, "I had to pay my dues; so does everyone else." If it wasn't said out loud, it was implied. If we couldn't get in the door to pay our dues, we weren't motivated enough to get ahead. The circumstances surrounding our birth — wealth or poverty, college education or high-school drop-out, family connections or violent dysfunction — didn't matter. At the most basic level, the circumstances do not absolve us from personal responsibility. We each made choices. But did we each have a full understanding of the choices available?

Even though the me generation shaped today's world, their self-focused ideas and beliefs no longer hold the weight they used to, and they shouldn't. We have more information today than yesterday; we have seen the results of self-absorbed insensitivity. It is time for ideas and beliefs to evolve too. And, it is important to take care and not throw out what worked as we create the new. We moved away from the basics in our quest for happiness. We didn't need the cruises and expensive clothes; they were an inadequate substitute for what was missing in our lives. The longer we drifted apart, the wider the separation and the greater the need to fill the gap with flashy substitutes. We bought our tickets and flew away on exotic vacations. Once there, the children rushed off to find adventure. Mom went in one direction and Dad headed off in still another. If we think about the times that truly satisfied, they were the moments of togetherness and simplicity, and of accomplishment that came at no one's expense. Ideas that promoted our separate success did not satisfy, and if the truth be told, never will. Our past is invaluable if we learn what supported us — what helped us grow into better human beings — as well as to understand what did not.

We are growing up! This is the beginning of a resurgence of radical honesty, natural integrity, and relaxed authenticity — a giant win for us all. As we lighten our grip on what we have known and hoped for, we learn from the emerging world events, and no longer sidestep the experience of interconnectedness. The world's economic, emotional, and physical distress naturally widens our ability to comprehend a growing dependence on each other. These lessons — like water carving a wall of rock — alter our perceptions and focus. As we integrate the lessons we automatically grasp the importance of balancing receiving with giving. Business practices once expected and accepted are seen for what they are — unthinkable — and far less than of what we are capable.

Today there are a few organizations ahead of the evolutionary curve. They are the precursors for what is to come. We don't have to wait for evolution to take place — look closely — it is already happening. In an article titled *Toyota forgoes layoffs despite plant closings* Lindsay Chappell, the bureau chief at Automotive News, writes:

> They will relearn how to pick up screws. They will study safety practices. They will take classes on workplace diversity and ethics, study corporate history, clean up the mess of urban vandals and probably even plant flowers.
>
> But one thing Toyota's 4,500 idled North American workers will not do is get laid off.
>
> As the U.S. auto industry sheds workers, and even Nissan offers buyouts, Toyota is sticking by its proud — and expensive — tradition of no layoffs during hard times.
>
> "This was the first chance we've really had to live out our values," said Latondra Newton, general manager of Toyota's team member development center in Erlanger, Ky. "We're not just keeping people on the payroll because we're nice. At the end of all this, our hope is that we'll end up with a more skilled North American work force."[5]

What does this unusual activity signal for organizations? It is not the end, but the beginning of great possibility. Today entire human resource departments, CEOs, VPs, managers and supervisors are constantly trying to find ways to engage people and hold them accountable. Substantial resources are dedicated to pay administration, the review process (when it is done), rewards and punishment of all types, training programs and seminars, anything and everything to motivate and drive results.

Imagine what it would mean when people are as invested in

each other's success, and that of the organization, as they are in their own. If they view their workplace as part of the solution, as an enlightened organization, or at the least one choosing to become enlightened, any objective is attainable. That workplace has the potential to become truly unstoppable. If though, awakening employees — including all levels within the organization — view their workplace as part of the problem, they have three choices: 1) Work from within to change the organization. 2) Leave and work for, or create one that is more enlightened. 3) Stay put; wither and die with the organization. Extinction is what happens during evolutionary cycles. We either evolve or we disappear.

To varying degrees people are awakening to a bigger vision. We resonate with new truths that, in actuality, are ancient truths reborn. The truth has always been present and available, even when few were able or willing to understand. Truth is both genuine and real. What is true today was true yesterday, and will be true tomorrow — individually, organizationally and globally. Those who are awakening to this understanding sense the rightness in finding honoring ways to work and be together.

Evolution of our species and our organizations cannot be stopped. What we are experiencing now is the forerunner of an extreme shift. As new individuals stand up for others as well as for themselves, the numbers of us willing to win at another's expense will fall. Good has a way of attracting more good. And feeling good is wonderful validation of one's actions. The act of sincerely being of use to each other creates an upward movement pulling us into ever-increasing desire to be of greater service. Once one makes even the smallest shift towards a more inclusive reason for being, the smaller *just-for-me* way of thinking feels like a tight pair of pants one can't wait to remove.

We are hard-wired to be in community. This sense of connection is the foundation for the success of a wide range of businesses from Amazon to Zappos. It also lies beneath the broad and continuously replicated success of Delancey Street, a San Francisco-based organization that understands the power of community. Belonging to something bigger than oneself is at the center of their success in working with ex-convicts and others among the disenfranchised. In the words of Delancey Street:

> "We're considered the country's leading residential self-help organization for substance abusers, ex-convicts, homeless and others who have hit bottom. Our average resident has been a hard-core drug addict for sixteen years, abusing alcohol and multiple drugs and has dropped out of school at the 7th grade and has been institutionalized several times. Many have been gang members; most have been trapped in poverty for several generations. Rather than hire experts to help the people with problems, we decided to run Delancey Street with no staff and no funding. Like a large family, our residents must learn to develop their strengths and help each other. It's an approach to changing lives that is 'against all odds'.
>
> We said we were going to take ex-convicts and ex-addicts and teach them to be teachers, general contractors, and truck drivers. They said it couldn't be done. We said we were going to take 250 people who had never worked and had no skills and teach them to build a 400,000 square foot complex as our new home on the waterfront. They said it couldn't be done. We said we were going to partner with colleges and get people who started out functionally illiterate to achieve Bachelor of Arts degrees. They said it couldn't be done. We said we were going to run successful restaurants, moving companies, furniture making, and cafés and bookstores without any professional help. They said it couldn't be done. We said we were going to do all this with no staff, no government funding, and no professionals. They laughed and said it couldn't be done.
>
> We struggle a lot but we've been doing it. For over 35 years we've been developing a model of social entrepreneurship, of education, of rehabilitation and change that is exciting and full of hope."

Being a part of something bigger opens our hearts and our capacity to contribute whether or not we are part of conventional society. Just the possibility of belonging invigorates us and readies us for change. Many of us are no longer willing to sell our souls or sacrifice another to get ahead. Some, the strong and solid amongst us, never were. They knew that success at someone else's expense came at too high a cost in discarded potential and shattered spirits.

When we choose ourselves alone, we feel it, and on many levels it reinforces our own unworthiness. The impact no longer hides from us. It is becoming all too obvious. We are more aware of the truth that what we do to others, we do to ourselves. Hurting others hurts us too. We are now sufficiently evolved to see the huge cost inherent in the suppression of others and of ourselves. The uncompromising idea of inclusion summons each of us into full expression of our unique talents and purpose. This higher under-standing is the ultimate in self-protection and self-service. In the words of Peter Block:

> "What we normally call problems (low performance, high costs, poor morale, unsafe streets, poor healthcare) are really symptoms of the breakdown of community."[6]

As more people are inspired by ever rising levels of consciousness, we work together in ways that build community rather than breaking it down. We work as one to heal the planet, and give ourselves and others, healthy ground to stand on, fresh water to drink and clean air to breath. It feels right. It feels good to be of use. In the process we realize our interconnectedness with each person. We can't rebuild our world by ourselves, nor do we want to work alone any longer. We see that we need each other, and begin to expand our sense of *me* to include *we*. Our self-concept gradually and naturally expands to include our community, our country and our world. As we see the impact of our financial decisions and pref-erences, our sense of self grows until at last we embrace each other.

We no longer need to populate the game board with winners and losers. If we stop the madness we will find answers to the crucial issues that have eluded mankind throughout history. Coming to terms with this is life-changing. It makes turning one's back on another impossible at best, and a consciously painful decision at worst, one that will haunt us until it rings so true it corrects our mistake. Evolution has been set into motion.

While evolution as a concept causes many disagreements in the realms of science and religion, it is certainly a concept that must be embraced if we intend to move our economy, our businesses and our lifestyles forward. As thinking, feeling, and responsible beings, it is time to come to terms with the need for conscious evolution — one that is not just of the mind, but consciously of the heart, and that moves us into inspired action.

Organizations alert to this changing evolutionary picture will appreciate the challenges involved in redesigning structures and processes to launch their own organizational evolution — for the good of the organization and its people, shareholders and stake-holders, society and for the good of planet Earth. They will see the opportunity inherent within the shift from *just me* to *we that includes me,* and the price of ignoring the invitation and signs of change. Evolution is always happening. Whether an organization chooses to consciously participate or not is actually voluntary. Although, electing to abstain is akin to standing on a railroad track as the freight train approaches.

Our future can be quite different from the challenging times at the turn of the 21st century. Those who choose to learn from the economic instability will also learn to adapt and thrive. With this wisdom we will have chosen evolution over extinction and a bold new future for generations yet to come. If we could look into a crystal ball and glimpse the new world heading right for us we would be astounded. The sheer wonder of it would stop our minds and end our conflicts with each other. In hindsight though, we may simply appreciate that evolution — a growing enlightenment of how we perform everyday workplace and life tasks — was really simple common sense.

The questions at the end of each chapter are designed to stimulate understanding and create inspired and actionable change within the organization. Use them for individual introspection, senior team visioning sessions, departmental or cross-functional team development, and as a checklist to un-limit organizational thinking and decision-making. For a richer and more robust understanding and integration, each question can be answered for the individual you and collectively from the standpoint of the organization.

Changing Workplaces

1. Make a list of changes currently impacting the organization.

2. Which of those changes could you have seen coming?

3. What changes present a significant paradigm shift?

4. How has the addition of younger workers changed the workplace?

5. What do you want from your workplace?

6. What do you believe others want from their workplace? How do you know your impression is accurate?

7. How important is meaningful work to you? To others?

8. What have you changed personally or organizationally as a result of your concern for yourself, others, or the planet?

9. What would it mean to the organization if people were as invested in the success of the organization as they are in their own success?

10. Think of a time when you left or considered leaving an organization in search of more enlightened practices? What was missing in the organization? What could have been different—culture, systems, business practices, structures, policies, or processes?

11. What is the difference in how you feel when you do

something that honors yourself and others rather than following self-interest alone? Consider a situation where there is or was a choice to create an *only you* solution or one that would also benefit others.

12.   What business structures or policies are built on a foundation of exclusion? What do you believe would happen if you redesigned the structures and policies with a foundation of inclusion? What organizational structures and policies are no longer as effective as they once were? What has contributed to those changes?

13.   In what areas is your organization particularly vulnerable to shifting paradigm? Talent acquisition and retention? Economic shifts? Creativity and innovation? Overall sustainability? Customer retention? Reputation? Cross cultural and generational influences? Impact of technology?

Chapter 2

The Change Conundrum

What is now proved was once only imagined.
— William Blake

The Belief Paradox

Change has most always been perceived as difficult. Humans seem to cling tooth and nail to the old, even when it is painful and proven inadequate. For the organization, just the words *change effort* frequently illicit unpleasant memories. Most of us have been involved in organizational attempts at change. Few were truly successful. Few, if any, actually gave us everything we sought. Slowly, sometimes not so slowly, we drifted back to old patterns of behavior and the new processes slipped between the cracks. Given enough time all evidence was wiped out except the emotional baggage created with the loss of time and resources. Millions, perhaps billions of dollars were used up in search of illusive change.

There is a reason change efforts are called the flavor of the month. Workplace change is no different than New Year's resolutions. We know something's not working and we need a change, like a diet and exercise program. The answer we land upon sounds good at the time. I personally purchased not one, but two exercise machines that ended up collecting dust. But before they did I climbed aboard regularly and perspired, right up to the day my schedule encountered a bump. A belief that I was someone who lacked time for exercise came into conflict with my need for change.

This is no different than what happens when a company decides to improve leadership skills. Good, maybe even great, training is developed. Inspiring seminars are completed. Books filled with valuable follow-up information find their way onto office shelves. Support groups are created. And then life happens. Deadlines, meetings, and old habits take over.

While a distraction, life happening is not the real reason meaningful change is so illusive. Why didn't the change take? What was it that got in the way? There were great programs, good materials, and logical ideas, yet little meaningful change resulted. Why was it so easy to return to the old ways even when the old ways weren't working all that well?

Minds are constantly comparing and contrasting and making decisions about what is true and what isn't. Normal decision-making is based upon old knowledge. We compare the idea being presented with what we already believe to be true. If there is enough old information to support the new idea, it is accepted. We continually build around old foundations. Truly radical ideas are less likely to be accepted unless they ring true intuitively. However, the business world struggles with concepts like intuition, so we habitually reject any hypothesis too different from our personal and collective beliefs, even when our immediate experience stands in stark contrast.

Much everyday decision-making isn't conscious. When presented with new ideas or possibilities something silent within us decides whether or not the idea presents safety or risk. This is an intensely personal process. It has nothing to do with the future of the organization or the worthiness of the idea. It has everything to do with our personal buttons, what we believe protects the secrets we carry and how to best maintain our status quo. We would not consider the need to connect with fellow workers if we spent most of our time making certain they didn't know who we really were.

Beliefs about humanity in general color our interactions and work ethics. If we feel those around us are unworthy of our time or that nothing will change as a result, that too will enter into our personal equation. It wouldn't necessarily be a conscious process. We would just reject the idea out-of-hand, unaware that one of our buttons had been pushed.

Meaningful change requires a shift in our belief systems, recognition that our beliefs are paradoxical to what we now see as true. In order to assimilate change in any significant way we must be willing to step into a space of not knowing the answer. As long as we know what is true, we can't see any other truth, regardless of its basis in fact. Allowing ourselves to not know is contrary to everything we have been taught since we were small children. Human minds are constantly working the problem, searching through memory banks of old material trying to find new solutions.

Many great solutions can only break through in a flash of insight. Our shields, composed of *what we believe to be true,* are normally deployed, so new ideas have to wait until we let our guards down. Insights wait for a widening of the space between thoughts, like shower moments when we are thoughtlessly present to the water's warm embrace. As soon as our guards drop the insights appears. When they do, especially when we aren't used to receiving them, they are often accompanied by a sense of wonder.

Change by the very nature of our tenacious beliefs is difficult. And, if we don't allow ourselves to change, evolution will eventually catch up with us. It caught up with the Swiss watch makers, typewriter companies, manufacturers of records, and cassettes. Now the list of casualties has grown to include producers of DVDs, several American car companies, well-known banks, and manufacturers of telephone equipment. History has much to teach us when we are willing to observe and learn.

Personally the evidence is in as well. Smokers faced with lung cancer often continue to smoke right up until they quit breathing permanently. We've all overhead people say, "It's my right to smoke." Only one in nine, when faced with a choice to change a habit or die, will succeed according to Alan Deutschman.[7] In Alan's talk at IBM's *Global Innovation Outlook* conference in 2004, this eye-opener unsettled many top executives with good reason. It didn't bode well for organizations attempting to create significant and lasting change.

Changing old habits is often viewed as a threat to personal identity. It is easier, the mind reasons, to die than change. We are fully invested in our beliefs even in the face of mounting evidence to the contrary. On a subconscious level we have bought into the notion that we are our ideas. After all, who are we if we are not our thoughts? A better question to ask would be, "Who are we without them?"

The obesity epidemic is another case in point. All we have to do is put down our spoons and forks but eating — many of us reason — gives life meaning. If we knew that a special diet would cure our ills, would we change? We all have things that we wouldn't want to give up, things that would make us healthier, but it is easier to rationalize and create stories in support of our vice than it is to break the habit. Perhaps that is what the dinosaurs in the children's storybooks thought as well, as the weather changed to rain and then to ice and they lost the ability to make further choices.

Seeing Through the Conundrum

1. Looking at past change efforts, how successful were they? Upon what did you base the idea of success?

2. How did you feel about the change effort?

3. How did others feel about the change effort? How do you know?

4. Did you personally change to the degree the organization desired? Why or why not? What internal changes would have been necessary to make the external changes stick? What support was provided? What support was utilized?

5. How do you feel when anyone tries to change you? Does it work? Do you change upon request?

6. What makes you want to change? What makes you actually change?

7. Have you experienced a flash of insight? What did you learn?

8. From where did the insight come?

9. What businesses in your industry are meeting with evolutionary challenges or are facing extinction?

10. What could they have done to change the course of their history? Why didn't they?

11. What extinction event is headed your way? Personally? Professionally?

12. What aren't you doing, or could you be doing, that would change the course of your personal or professional history? What keeps you from taking action?

13. Who would you be (or not be) if you were to make the changes in #12? What identity is most comfortable...or most unfamiliar?

Chapter 3

Radical Honesty – What It Is and Isn't

Our lives improve only when we take chances - and the first and most difficult risk we can take is to be honest with ourselves.

— Walter Anderson

Owning Our Stories

Our continued storytelling is fueled by the energy of our beliefs. We add to our stories with each new experience. In the workplace, we bring our old stories with us and create new ones with each passing day. These stories tell us how to act towards each other, what behavior is safe and what is not, and who to trust. They tell us when to keep our mouths closed and our ideas to ourselves, as well as how important it is to be on time, to be successful, or to work hard. Our stories are our personal guidance systems. They tell us whether it's best to carefully navigate around organizational landmines or to plow right through.

We walk into new jobs full of hope, yet limited by our stories. Watch as new hires start their first day. Under the nervousness you find hope. Some hope to find a place to fit in and to learn new skills. Others look for friendly acceptance and connection. None of us consciously look for boredom or mental abuse. Instead, we hope to find a sense of safety, a place where we can settle in, set down roots and grow. We may also hope to hide the truth about ourselves, worried that our co-workers will discover that we are frauds and that we don't really belong there. When we are aware enough, many of us will find this last hope. Hope is intricately linked to our sense of worth. Even what we are willing to hope for has been embedded within us before we walk in the door.

We cross the thresholds of our new workplaces with our past successes and failures. Amid a new job, in a new place, with new people, our stories are not new. According to the Aberdeen Group's 2006 Benchmark Study,[8] 86 percent of respondents agree that employees make their decision whether or not to stay with a company within the first six months on the job. Everything we have encountered — life with our families and friends, pre-school through university, and every job since — is written into our consciousness.

These experiences translate into our expectations about our futures. They tell us how the business world works. They create our understanding about what we need to do to get ahead, to stay safe within the pack, or to merely survive. And, at some level, we have already decided where we will fall on the success scale, by means of our worldview, and of ourselves within it. All of this goes into our decision to stay and contribute, or to offer our talents and insights elsewhere, a loss on many levels. The real cost of turnover is high. Estimates run from $10,000 per turnover to 150 percent of the employee's annual compensation package.[9] It is definitely not pocket change.

These stories write the future of organizations before the vision, goals, and ensuing actions take place. They determine whether or not the organization will wildly succeed, apparently succeed, stay afloat, or sink quickly and painfully into oblivion. A talented and discerning observer can tell instantly, just by watching with an eye to both subtle and overt individual and organizational programming, what stories are polluting the organization's future. It is actually quite easy once you know where to look.

The extent of fear's pervasiveness will determine how long an organization has before it begins to implode. Fear is viral in nature and begins eating away confidence. It replaces the willingness to create anew with stagnant complacency. When it is present the organization is much more comfortable in the known, basing all their thoughts and theories on what has come before, unable or unwilling to leap into a different future. They will see the future rushing at them like a bull charging a matador, and stand right in the middle of their past programming, unconsciously awaiting the end.

In stagnant organizations words like honesty, integrity, and truth are hollow. They have to be. When fear, doubt and worry are in charge they speak; they communicate; they set the meaning in the workplace; they determine the acceptability of unacceptable business practices and drive the resultant actions. Fractional and self-protected thinking, inadequacy and its twin — arrogance, restricted input resulting in even more constricted solutions, stress, rivalry and greed are the uninspired and unsurprising outcomes.

Dollar bills line the halls and cover the floors of our organizations. When we are immersed in worry and doubt we walk right past them. These bills are the new ideas that reinvent our businesses. They are the flash of insight that results in unexpected answers to problems. They are the Post-It Note, penicillin, the microwave, champagne, the pacemaker, Super Glue and the ice cream cone — all brilliant ideas that would have been missed if someone had not seen the potential. Every moment of every day we can reach down and fill our pockets with a freshly minted currency. Unexpected wealth is always available whether we see it or not. Rather than worrying about increasing financial uncertainty, it is rewarding to consider widening our focus enough to see the opportunities we overlook.

The founders of Workplace Evolution learned this lesson from their partner at VPI Strategies. Sherri Petro recognized genius in her son's hockey coach. She always felt that his day job, driving a truck, didn't come anywhere near to tapping into his unique mind. It wasn't that driving a truck was a bad job; it was just the wrong job for him. Andrej is from the Czech Republic. His use of the English language is good, not great, and he speaks with a definite accent. Andrej is one of the millions of well-educated and personally motivated immigrants who are under-employed in the United States.

Sherri could see potential. She followed her inner knowing and spoke honestly to him about her observations. Thank goodness she did. Andrej's contribution to this book as our research assistant changed much of the content on these pages. His international insight, his brilliant and unconventional thinking, led me to reassess ideas and expand my use of language. Had Sherri conformed to conventional thinking or chosen to stay silent she would have walk right past Andrej's potential. She knew that in order to move beyond time-worn behavior, a renaissance of understanding was required.

The first step is the Ah-Ha! Of course this is what's happening. Recognizing that we create our worlds with our stories gives us the opportunity to change our world by choosing differently. Choice is not just a matter of what we do. It is also about who we choose to be. If we concentrate only on what we do, the beliefs and thoughts that determine our actions will eventually take over again. We will then find ourselves doing what appears to be different, driven by the same stories, moving towards the same unproductive end.

Bona fide choice is not laden with unseen beliefs and stories. And, such unhampered choice allows us to evolve consciously. Evolutionary organizations will face a far different future. Words such as honesty, integrity, and truth will have a radically different meaning, and elicit a significantly different response inside and outside the organization. These new organizations won't steal the headlines with their illegal and immoral exploits, and be met with skepticism and disgust. They will be an integral part of a larger solution. These companies will do good work alongside other enlightened organizations and help create a better quality of life for us all.

As we evolve we can see that as we reject anyone due to our beliefs about them or ourselves, we enter into judgment and negativity, and that directly affects us. Every action, thought, or word has harmful or useful consequences. If we choose to, we can recognize the difference between what supports us and what doesn't, and come back to what is good and decent.

Meetings are crucial to project-specific and overall communication. In spite of that meetings are often ineffective. It is easy to tell if a meeting will be productive by the quality of interactions. Generally when tempers flare, or when people are passive and resigned, or need to feel important, little is said and productivity is lost. We push through, sometimes making decisions, sometimes not. To everyone present, the meeting's dysfunction is obvious. What isn't so obvious is that this meeting just reinforced lower expectations for the next one. Chances are that future meetings will miss their potential too. A progressive option would be to create agreements that wisely oblige us to call out behaviors that defeat us. In this way we can create a culture that addresses damaging behaviors and sets an expectation of genuine participation.

Evolutionary organizations will grow to wholly appreciate that reaching their full potential includes creating a culture of radical honesty. Without bona fide choice, we fail to understand honesty, and we fail ourselves and our organizations. As we take steps towards understanding the power of straightforward conversations and act in ways that infuse honesty into the workplace, our ability to create sustainable businesses increases exponentially. The initial proof of this premise lies in how it feels. As we tell the truth earnestly, with compassion for all the old stories, our backbones straighten and we stand taller in the knowledge that we have claimed the courage to unravel our stories and reach our full potential.

Personal and Organizational Honesty

1.   What workplace stories limit unstoppable success?

2.   What personal stories limit your ability to wildly succeed?

3.   What was the last thing you should have said at work that you didn't?

4.   What was the cost of that choice?

5.   What was the last thing you should have said at home that you didn't?

6.   What was the cost due to your decision?

7.   In what ways have you seen fear used as a management, marketing or hiring and retention tactic?

8.   How much time does your organization spend analyzing the past as a basis for creating the future?

9.   Is what you believe possible based on past failure and success?

10. What decisions have you or the organization made lately that feel uncomfortable or that you felt were unobtainable? What organizational belief systems lay beneath the decisions?

11. Looking at your organization's decision-making process, is it primarily defensive, offensive or a hybrid?

Chapter 4

Out of the Rut

Little progress can be made by merely attempting to repress what is evil; our great hope lies in developing what is good.

— Calvin Coolidge

Free of Fear and Outdated Beliefs

How then does one break free of old programming and outdated beliefs, and get to that place where one can make decisions consciously, without undue influence of old fears and failures? Simply stated, it starts with a decision to see more clearly — to gain appreciation of the personal decision-making process. This in turn, leads to a working understanding of how the collective of individuals drives the organization.

The initial adjustment involves a willingness to see the thoughts that silently sabotage us and our companies. With this correction, the thoughts standing in the way of conscious decision-making, for both individuals and organizations, begin to appear. This is no different than deciding to buy a new car and instantly seeing your car of choice everywhere you go. It is a basic element of awareness. Attention is now focused on seeing. Before the decision to see clearly, negative and unproductive thoughts would have slipped in, done their damage, and disappeared unnoticed.

Once we begin looking we get small glimpses, larger impressions, and at times feel as if a full-on assault has begun. The small glimpses are obviously the easiest to miss, and often offer the greatest win. These are so tiny that, if we aren't alert, the opportunity to learn from them is missed altogether. This is not unlike stepping from the shower in all our naked glory. As we walk past the full-length mirror, we catch the briefest flash of our body. In that second, our minds make a judgment. Since the overwhelming majority of us don't want to hear our mind's judgment about our physiques, we quickly turn away and edit our thought. If we are quick enough, we can convince our conscious mind that we didn't hear or see anything at all. Unfortunately, our subconscious knows what it saw and heard.

We get these same small glimpses in the workplace. They actually happen all the time. At work we edit our judgments about others, such as the likelihood of the conversation with the boss going well, and our real thoughts about projects and new directions. A running conversation exists within our head. Depending on the study, anywhere from 83 percent to 98 percent of those internal conversations are negative. We are better at digging the hole deeper, than giving ourselves a hand-up. With all the inner chatter it is amazing that anything constructive gets accomplished. We wonder about what the person sitting next to us makes, and what it means about our worth and the other guy's. When we speak up, we quickly craft stories about what we should have said and worry about the competency judgments those within earshot surely made. These conversations are unending. They don't begin to slow until we begin to observe them. The very act of observing starts the pendulum swinging. It is as if these thoughts are errant children and all of a sudden they become aware that a grown-up is watching.

Whether the thoughts we see come in a glimpse or full-color motion pictures, it is time to stop and watch. At first, we don't need to do anything but be curious. These thoughts hold conscious decision-making hostage, so we want to know everything about them. If we were held captive we would carefully watch our captor. This is no different.

It is common when we begin to see our thoughts, to judge ourselves for having them. Rather than adding more fuel to the thought process, just watch. When you see one just observe that it's interesting, without labeling it good or bad. It is interesting if we are curious. It is just a thought, nothing more. Labeling a thought is our mind's way of taming it and putting it safely into a known category. We miss the opportunity to see the details once we label a thought. Labeling stops the process, so resist the temptation to control and observe instead. Let curiosity guide you.

Just as a good host is hospitable when a guest shows up at the door, when thoughts show up invite them in. Offer them a seat and be gracious. The immediate urge will be to attempt to change the thought. The urge is a thought too, so just watch it. The more attention a thought is given, the more its presence is resisted, the greater its staying power. If we just invite it in, neither wanting it to stay or leave, like a good guest, it will leave before we know it. Of course, behaving like a good host in order to get the thought to leave is actually engaging. Regrettably, doing something without authenticity, in order to get something to happen is manipulation, and it doesn't work. Authenticity of action is a cosmic law designed to keep us honest and humble. Gurus, mystics, meditation teachers, and practitioners, not to mention countless others with years of consciousness training and practice, can testify to this fact.

Dive into the game. Make it into a grand experiment, a little game of hide and seek, and keep inviting your thoughts to appear. The better we are at stopping, being curious and hospitable, the more visible our decision-making process becomes. Experiment individually and organizationally. Make it into a grand game. Play with it. Talk about it and share your insights. Be collectively interested and amazed at your minds' creative license. Not everyone is talking about us when we think they are. That's one example of imagination creating reality. When we talk openly about thoughts and fears, they are tugged out of their hiding places and lose their power. Keeping them tucked inside is uncomfortable and guarantees their uninterrupted dominion.

As each of us, and our organizations, get comfortable with the basics of thought awareness we can all go hunting for harmful and limiting beliefs. During the hunt we begin to notice themes and, not surprisingly, they will all be fear-based. In the words of Franklin D. Roosevelt,[10] "...The only thing we have to fear is fear itself," so we can't let fear deter us. Acknowledging fear doesn't make us weak; it makes us strong when we turn and face it. The people who told us there weren't any monsters in the closet were wrong. The monsters are there, inside our stories and pictures of what is possible. The good news is they won't harm us; they just want out.

To help open the closet door it is important to understand seven universal myths[11] or fears. Most all of our negativity (and much of what appears to be positive) fits into one or more of seven categories:

1. The world is a scary place.
2. There is not enough.
3. The power is outside of us.
4. We are not enough.
5. There is one right way.
6. We know what is real.
7. We are separate and alone.

The categories can be used like binoculars, to help find the hidden pictures. With a little practice, we can see a thought, and in the same moment understand which myth is in control. Each one of us is influenced by all seven universal myths, as are our organizations. We tend to mask our thoughts, the supporting evidence we gather, as well as our underlying motivation, in order to bolster our right to hang onto them. This is not intentional. It is however, automatic — a completely programmed impulse. Our responsibility is to bring care-filled awareness to our automatic behaviors.

Seeing through our tactics can be very entertaining once we get the hang of it. The categories are useful tools for discerning what is real and true, and what is merely the weaving of personal story. They help us peel away the many layers, rather like opening a Russian Matryoshka doll. As you open it a smaller doll is revealed. In the case of our hunt for limiting beliefs, rather than decreasing in size, each successive story will be of increasing importance.

Once we are more adept at seeing our personal thoughts, we can spot those that limit our organizations, because the same stories are playing out in the workplace. This is quite natural since they are the macro (collective) of the micro (individuals). The organization's decision-making process is clouded by a jumble of beliefs in the same way the individual's is clouded. When the organization becomes willing and committed to uncovering the thoughts and fears enabling habitual decisions, it has the possibility of becoming an enlightened organization.

The seven myths, adapted from Campbell, Gregory and Johnson's *The Grand Experiment,* are invaluable tools for organizations. Vision, structures, controls, decision-making models, in fact, every aspect of organizational life, is controlled by collective beliefs. These beliefs dictate our actions and lead us to respond in predictable and reactive ways in the workplace. Look carefully at the behaviors for evidence of the beliefs' dominance within your organization. Then, envision the potential once the myths are deconstructed.

Myth #1: The world is a scary place

— Culture: protect and defend, exposure-avoidance, negative world view, command and control, crisis driven, risk management, closed-door power structure, policy constrained

— Behaviors: controlling processes, micro-managing, defensiveness, denying, hiding, inflexibility, secretive, guarding information, assuming and expecting the worst, reacting prematurely without complete information

— Possibilities: self-awareness, seeing what is, honesty, truth, openness, engagement, conscious choice, personal responsibility, clarity, personal growth and workplace development, expansive visions

Myth #2: There is not enough

— Culture: competition for scarce resources, win-lose, survival mentality, struggle, containment strategies for time, money and resources, stockpiling

— Behaviors: withholding, back-stabbing, pressuring results, perceiving lack and limitation, repression, greed, physical and emotional burn-out, hoarding resources, begrudging time spent

— Possibilities: collaboration, strategic alliances, playing together, abundance thinking, generosity, sharing, teaming, cross-training, transparency, creative use of resources

Myth #3: The power is outside of us

— Culture: oppression, apathy, risk-aversion, yes people, concentrated power, self-suppression

— Behaviors: victimhood, disengagement, blaming, deferring, sabotaging, manipulating, anger, frustration, entitlement

— Possibilities: personal responsibility and accountability, job contentment, genuine empowerment, a personal stake in success, self-driven productivity improvement, co-created innovative solutions, leading during change, anything is possible mindset

Myth #4: We are not enough

— Culture: perfectionism, uncertainty, arrogance and judgment (both of self and other), performance paralysis, corruption, secrecy

— Behaviors: angst and self-abuse, lack of self-trust, self-doubt, failure to verbalize and concretize new ideas, projecting self-doubt onto others — seeing them as not enough, resistance to goals, expectations and feedback, underperforming, work-a-holism

— Possibilities: authenticity, flexibility, self-trust, trust of others, fearless engagement, responsive relationships, compassionate and nurturing work environments, working from one's strengths, high performing individuals and teams, feedback immediacy, stretching towards larger goals

Myth #5: There is one right way

— Culture: turf wars, creativity killers, resistance to change, micro-management, strangulation by policy, individual and organizational paralysis, warring opinions

— Behaviors: inability or unwillingness to delegate, closed minds, concentrating power, emphasizing why things can't be done, basing decisions on should, short-sightedness, inflexibility, tunnel-vision, discriminating, agenda-based communicating, long-standing conflicts

— Possibilities: creativity, emphasis on how, solution focused, inspired by diversity, visionary and ahead-of-the-curve thinking, organizational flexibility, bold risk-taking, respect and appreciation, idea collaboration, diversity-inspired solutions

Myth #6: We know what's real

— Culture: quantitative focus, supposition, predictability, evidence-based discovery, stressed creativity and innovation

— Behaviors: arrogance, thinking and acting traditionally, inability to see beyond the known, unwillingness to push limits or question, failure to see new possibilities or what's coming

—   Possibilities: learning, opportunity orientation, honoring of the intuitive, diversity of opinions and ideas, naturally expanding comfort zones, radical growth, hotbed of innovation and creativity, products and services that open new markets, adaptability to change, long-term success

Myth #7: We are separate and alone

—   Culture: dispiritedness, disconnection, small-thinking, me-focused, irrelevance, loss of meaning, mediocrity, debilitating stress

—   Behaviors: cynicism, aggressive, competitive, ineffective team players, arrogance, stressed out, resigned, checked out, overwhelmed, alienated, unmotivated, desperation to belong

—   Possibilities: aligned purpose, living the mission, sense of shared purpose, investment in something bigger than oneself, inexhaustible potential, powerful community, robust health, positive impact on society, personal, professional and organizational transformation

The choice is always up to each of us. Our decisions validate the decisions, regardless of the wholeness or fragmentation, of the communities and organizations in which we invest our time, talent and treasury. We are always choosing whether to be influenced by outdated, programmed beliefs and thoughts, or to move into more evolved behaviors. Evolution is happening. Many of us are choosing to move beyond the limitation of fears. Fearless people will find job contentment in fearless organizations. They will seek out contemporaries unwilling to suppress themselves or to suppress the talents of others. Fearless individuals, even those who have just started down the path, already are choosing to work with evolving people in evolving organizations to further their own development.

In the past our belief in the myths has handcuffed us to obsolete business structures. As we break free of the myths' influence we also find the courage to cut ties that limit us in any way. Freedom is an aphrodisiac. Once one gets a taste of freedom, there is no way to forget its flavor. From that moment forward every new experience will be compared to that taste — to the sensation of freedom.

Fearlessness becomes the new baseline even though at first, the thought of it may scare us. As the numbers grow, and more individuals break free from fear's control, the snowball begins to roll downhill, picking up speed and sweeping us along in its avalanche. Fear creates more fear. Its end product is conformity. Fearlessness too, brings with it a type of conformity, only this conformity doesn't constrict; it expands. Fearlessness encourages greater fearlessness.

This is great news for organizations willing to evolve. Their budding potential energizes their workforce and magnetically draws others who tire of fear. Freed energy previously burned up warding off doubt and worry, channels into imagination fueling new ideas and driving market-altering products and services. An *anything-is-possible* mentality awaits organizations courageous enough to consciously choose evolution, to take the quantum leap. This is more than a pipe dream. We have been limited in our thinking by our fears. Once we drop from fear's influence, a world of new possibilities emerges.

Breaking Free of Limitation

1.   What are the themes of unspoken conversations within the workplace?

2.   In what ways does *The World is a Scary Place* define mission, vision, and values?

3.   In what ways does *There is Not Enough* hamper problem solving, collaboration, strategic planning, strategic alliances, and training and development?

4.   In what ways does *The Power is Outside of Us* impact productivity and overall sustainability, the success of recent change initiatives and leadership at all levels?

5.   In what ways does *We Are Not Enough* keep us or others from contributing our best and limit involvement and risk taking?

6.   In what ways does *There is One Right Way* impact innovation, creativity and the heart of the organization?

7.   In what ways does *We Know What is Real* limit the organization's thought process and ability to compete in the marketplace?

8.   In what ways does *We Are Separate and Alone* drive the decision-making process and create silo thinking and behaviors within the organization? In our relationships with customers, vendors, competitors and our communities?

9.   What is your workplace's untapped potential and how can you and your organization tap into it?

10. What is your organization capable of once everyone within it chooses to see and acknowledge the myths rather than being determined by them?

11. How could you and your organization integrate myth awareness?

12.   What risks are apparent in such an endeavor?

13.   What are you inspired to do differently in your organization based on your insights and answers?

Chapter 5

Assessing the Risk

There came a time when the risk to remain tight in the bud was more painful than the risk it took to blossom.

— Anais Nin

Risky business

Movement in a new direction may feel risky. It can also feel exhilarating. Any change brings with it an element of chance, and some of us are more comfortable with risk than others. Regardless of our risk tolerance, deciding to explore our myths and fears brings with it a bit of trepidation. We think we might find things we don't want to see. That concern is not just a fear. It is what will actually happen — and that's a good thing. We have stuffed all of the things we didn't want to see or feel into the recesses of our minds, thinking it was the best way to protect ourselves. It wasn't. Although at the time it seemed like a pretty good idea. All those things we stuffed are in control now, and are the foundations of the stories. They keep us on a tight, short leash, unable to be honest — even with ourselves.

Until we are willing to stand up and be counted for what we see as true, our beliefs are paper tigers, imitations of the real thing. These tigers though, have real teeth, biting us every time we deny

39

what we know in our hearts. They hurt us when we verbally stand down as well as when we let our silence speak. From a personal standpoint, denial is convincing evidence that we lack conviction and proves we are sad imposters. It hurts us personally and numbs us to each other when we are not aligned with integrity and honor. Organizationally it translates into an ever-widening drain of potential, passion and commitment.

So much is lost with the inability to be heard and to be counted for a higher integrity, an innocent purpose. The personal loss is obvious, but the loss to the world where we spend enormous amounts of time and energy — our workplace — is not quite as visible. While not easily quantifiable, it is of great consequence. Aversion to risk minimizes our contribution and ability to effect change. We make ourselves and the companies where we work, victims of our stories. In the process we lose the ability to capitalize on the synergy of great minds working together in pursuit of something only the visionaries among us have dared dream. In this emergent time of yes we can, we risk that nothing will change. We decide. Change will happen when we are willing to shamelessly question the existence of any policy, rule or structure that limits us. It will occur as we step outside of accepted norms, to push the limits, and birth something truly new.

This principle is important to us individually and organiza-tionally. We all possess portions of the larger picture. When we remain silent, what is created in the end is fraught with absent potential in the form of quality issues, design flaws, consumer disinterest and ensuing reputation repair. The importance of engaged employees can not be understated.

"In North America, fewer than one in three (only 29 percent) of employees are fully engaged, and 19 percent are actually disen-gaged...the study also found a strong correlation between employee engagement and retention. Moreover, the study found that engaged employees stay for what they can contribute (they like their work), while disengaged employees stay for what they

can get (job security, favorable job conditions, and growth opportunities). The picture in the UK and Ireland is slightly worse;
there less than one in four (23 percent) employees is fully
engaged and nearly as many are actually disengaged."[12]

As we come together, sharing our understanding and learning
from each other, a fuller picture emerges. Combining our skills and
knowledge, more solutions are readily available. It is as though we
get license to additional sections of the universal knowledge bank.
When one of us stands alone it is not as powerful as when two, or
thirty, or even better, four hundred stand ready. It isn't just the sum
of the parts. What is created is greater than the sum. It is exponential.
Standing together, for each other, we open an access point into possibility that will not open to us alone. We do indeed need each other,
and the reasons are larger than what the mind can comprehend.

When we feel stuck and weary, all we have to do is look to the
people we admire for inspiration — Mother Teresa, Martin Luther
King, Jr., John F. Kennedy, Albert Einstein, Helen Keller, Franklin
D. Roosevelt, Billy Graham, Pope John Paul II, Eleanor Roosevelt,
Winston Churchill. The list goes on.[13] These are the people who, still
today, warm our hearts and capture our imaginations. It is sometimes
hard to see that those we admire are individuals just like us. The only
difference is they were willing to be counted, to step up and be heard.
We admire their ability to take the risk and that they stood for
something beyond themselves. They chose their commitment.

In that way we are like them. Each decision we make, each
action we take speaks to our commitment, conscious or not. Our
bodies tell us when we are aligned with our true beliefs and deep
commitments, if we are willing to listen. We are either committed
to each other, or to ourselves. When we don't choose the whole
there is an immediate loss — a recognizable ache — and it comes
in the form of a knot in the middle of the abdomen. It gnaws at us
and appears to leave when we distract ourselves and divert our
attention to something else. It doesn't leave. It becomes a more
ferocious monster in our belly.

Organizationally the proof is coming in too. If we look at the banking fiasco, we see that a controlling minority gained considerable wealth at a high cost to those less powerful. That is, until it began to implode at the top. Even so, huge bonuses continued, along with larger-than-life salaries, extravagant purchases and zero accountability. The banking industry is not alone in this shame. It took powerful corporate and government alliances, and compliant citizens for such a drama to play out. With the game tilted towards the few, we all lose. Americans alone lost two trillion in their workplace retirement plans in 15 months,[14] threatening the security of millions. The fallout will continue into many tomorrows. Time will tell what greater losses are still in store for us all.

The hierarchy of king and serf was never intended to optimize potential. It served a single purpose: to fill the coffers of the king. Survival of the serf wasn't required. Granted, it was a rather short-sighted model. Serf success should have meant more pennies for the king's coffers and appeasement of the king's ever-hungrier appetites. But, thriving serfs didn't mean more pennies for the king. It meant the king's soldiers weren't doing their job, that they had gone soft or gotten lazy.

This was the model of the times, one step along the evolutionary path. If we look carefully at the economic implosion we will see that this ancient model survives today in a slightly different form. We seem to have gotten stuck, repeating mistakes like the character in the movie *Ground Hog Day,* living this step over and over. At this 21st century tipping point, as company after company fails, there are not enough investors left to support the Ponzi scheme. Eventually, the failure of the serf equates to the failure of the king. Bernie Madoff, once a poster boy for Wall Street and the Ponzi king, is now the poster boy for the extreme effects of self-serving behaviors. The resulting fallout in dollars and suffering sadly testifies to the point.

A healthy alternative that releases the monster in our belly is opening wide enough to hear what we are genuinely committed to and speaking in support of that commitment. It means taking the risk to say what we really think and feel, and aligning with the truth that lies beneath the fear. The monster is made of fear. It is not shameful. It is nothing to feel bad about. It is there to help us, not to stop us in our tracks. It is there to show us the way into clarity, to show us when we are functioning from limitation. Its fierceness tells us we are being short-sighted and selfish. It is present when we are acting from fear rather than from the bigger picture of shared well-being and mutual interest.

When we speak from a place of commitment to each other, our words will not cause harm to ourselves or others. Doubt is absent and we feel good about ourselves and our world. We know that our word is priceless, that trusting ourselves and working together is what life is all about. We even know that any other choice begins the slide into doubt, into the wounded mind, body and spirit. Once we bring our choices into conscious awareness, the shift into limiting beliefs becomes less automatic. Seeing the beliefs triggers an opportunity to choose our commitment to each other again, and to heal the rifts that have separated us. It presents an opening into the remembrance that we can be one of those we admire.

What we do for the whole lifts us all upward into our shared potential. It does take a planet to save a village. For what good is there in saving the village when the lights in the world around it flicker and go dark. Imagine your workplace without consumers for your product or service, without vendors to supply your needs, without a purpose for being, without new blood and new ideas. None of us lives in a vacuum. Each of us has his or her role to play. If any one of us stands down, we all lose. John Donne's words say it well.

"No man is an Island, entire of itself; every man is a piece of the Continent, a part of the main; if a clod be washed away by the sea, Europe is the less, as well as if a promontory were, as well as if a manor of thy friends or of thine own were; any man's death diminishes me, because I am involved in Mankind; And therefore never send to know for whom the bell tolls; It tolls for thee."

Risk or Self-Interest?

1.   What do you believe would happen if you began thinking about the good of the whole in your decision-making processes?

2.   What do you believe you would lose or risk if you honor others?

3.   What makes you feel good about yourself that has staying power or that lasts, unlike a vacation, a new car, or a perfect haircut?

4.   What is the true cost of poverty, war, ever-present illness, or the lack of long-term success?

5.   Whom do you truly admire in the world today? What traits do they have?

6.   Imagine a world that takes care of all its citizens. What would it be like to be a part of creating that world?

7.   What are you genuinely committed to? How do you know what is possible? On what do you base your future scenarios or possibilities?

8.   If you knew you could create anything you could imagine, what would you do?

9.   What do you lose if you fail?

10.   What do you gain by trying regardless of result?

11.   What do we all win if you succeed?

12.   What is the bigger risk, failing or not trying?

13.   What would your answer be if you knew that an evolutionary shift from self-centered individuality to all-inclusive uniqueness, where individuality is enhanced not lost, was taking place?

14.   Are you willing to bet against evolution? What costs would you incur by losing the bet?

Chapter 6

Centering for the Evolving Workplace

Just as the wave cannot exist for itself, but is ever a part of the heaving surface of the ocean, so must I never live my life for itself, but always in the experience which is going on around me.

— Albert Schweitzer

Moving Beyond Fractions into Holistic Thinking

There are many vantage points from which to view the newly emerging world. Each point offers the prospect of full engagement for us as individuals and for our respective organizations. When we let go of knowing how things should look, anything becomes possible. We find unique ways to be in service to each other, developing new, uncommon associations. Playing not to lose prevents us from seeing competitors as alliances and vendors as part of our team. With conscious evolution all the rules change. Time is spent developing partners and learning how to share more freely, instead of trying to manipulate the system.

Sometime during the 20th Century, between the baby boom and the dot-com bust, we lost our way. Our identity became entangled with what we consumed rather than being an intrinsic outcome of our connections with our communities and society as a whole. Our social contract devolved into a contract of one.

A new social contract that focuses on renewed community is vitally important today. It is no longer possible to deny our interconnectedness. That idea was tough to sell not that long ago. Today, all we have to do is open our eyes and watch the dominos fall — housing market … banks … access to credit … lay-offs. It is now obvious that we are all connected. A social contract based upon this reality is ready for each of our signatures. Inspired by such a contract, the questions surrounding unconscionable salaries and mega-bonuses for failure dissolve. The short-term thinking that created them gives ways to a longer and wider view. If we had been thinking long-term, looking forward many generations into the future, we would have never entertained devastating practices or made such narrow decisions.

In a McKinsey study in 2007[15] 99 percent of executives responding said that large corporations make contributions to the public good. While the overwhelming majority saw the contribution primarily as job-creation, product and service, or innovative technological or scientific breakthroughs, it nonetheless indicates movement in a positive direction. Fifteen percent and 13 percent respectively, saw philanthropy or volunteer work within communities as important contributions to the public good. Regardless of how we define social responsibility, as we saw with the scandal involving the Peanut Corporation of America, social irresponsibility can be deadly for organizations and the societies in which they intend to thrive.

A shift in focus, moving beyond fractions and factions, to holistic thinking, is basic to redefining the social contract and redirecting attention. Rather than focusing on tasks and goals, it is time to shift gears and discover our workplaces' core meaning. The core is beyond product or service. It answers the question, "Who do we choose to be?" The answer has the potential to change just about everything within the workplace. This broader meaning, defined collectively by each organization, garners support and builds undeniable momentum.

Making this shift is evolutionary for the workplace. Establishing a central meaning is transformational. And, when the core meaning results in greater caring for the world and her citizens, it creates a rallying point from which aligned processes and decisions occur naturally. This point gives meaning to work and builds community in which all engage, learn and grow, and discover how to push limits. With this shift, there is reason to stretch and reach past old thinking, past limitation, into *man on the moon* innovation and creativity. This new meaning becomes the centering practice for the organization and stands as a sentinel embedded with the vision.

Working in the Now – Entering the Present Moment

Even with a clearly defined core meaning, it is easy to get distracted by thoughts about old failures and successes. Picture your thoughts as points on a continuum. The continuum spirals up and down from a center point called neutral. Each thought comes to rest at its appropriate spot on the spiral and pulls us upward into higher purpose or downward into a lesser one. As more points accumulate above the neutral point, being positive becomes easier. It is as if the amassed positive energy engages a magnet that attracts more positivity. The same is true of those thoughts that come to rest below the neutral point. The more we stay in negativity or positivity the more likely we will remain there, and the more difficult it becomes to change our course.

Baseball provides a good illustration. It's the bottom of the ninth inning and the home team is one out away from the league championship. The local coach stops the game and walks out to the mound, and tells his already stressed pitcher, "Whatever you do, do not throw an inside pitch. This batter can kill an inside pitch." If you have ever told yourself not to do something, you know how hard it is to do anything else. Thoughts complete themselves in action and the mind doesn't seem to understand the word *not*. Of course, you know how the story ends — one pitch, one home-run.

Understanding this concept is helpful. While all positive and negative thoughts are diversions, a little creative playtime for the mind, our negative ones do the most obvious damage. Because of this, the negative thoughts are the easiest and most important to spot. We can use them to help us enter present moment thinking, which is a key to individual and organizational success.

We are either in the present moment or we are engaged in our recollections of the past and dreams for the future. Actions take place in this moment, the now. There are many reasons to practice staying in *what is,* for one, it is the only true reality. Past and future do not actually exist in the present moment. They exist only in our minds, making them the ultimate day dream. They are mere imagination, no different than a child's make-believe tea party. Yet, we spend hours every day wrapped in our stories, comparing today to tomorrow or to what happened yesterday.

The present moment is also an access point into creativity and flow. When we are outside of it, we are spinning in thoughts. Moments of insight happen in the now as do experiences of being in the flow. Athletes at the top of their game enter the flow. It is that moment when time stands still and every move is graceful perfection. My son the skateboarder describes flow as the moment when the board, the skate park and the skater become one, a magical place where falling is impossible and he can pull off any trick he wishes. We find the same moments of flow in the workplace. If you've ever lost complete track of time while immersed in a project you loved, or worked with inspired teammates who could finish each others sentences and whose creative genius poured like water from a spring, you were inside the flow.

When we are present, we narrow the gap between mental activity and action, between seeing and doing. When thought gets in the way we doubt our natural abilities. Had the pitcher been focused on the present moment, rather than in the future worrying about the pitch, his training and talent would have taken over and the team would have been champions.

Our business mind also likes to spend time in the past and future, creating scenarios, crafting plans and conducting analysis. It can be useful, but only if done consciously, in full understanding of what is lost when we step out of the present moment. We can recognize and honor the past, but living there is not productive. Putting too much faith in the past, using it as comparison for today, limits us severely. It inadvertently hands over the colossal potential of each new moment to little more than memory. This moment is full of grace. The habit of living and working outside of it enables limitation. The reality is that today is not, nor has it ever been, limited by yesterday. Each moment stands on its own in all the possibility and potential of the universe.

Any thing is possible when we write upon the blank page of each new moment. We can find new answers for previously unanswerable questions. We can find them standing right here, right now — in the only moment that is — emptied of knowing and filled with a willingness and bold desire to learn.

The habit of linear thinking keeps us locked in a never-changing dance. Change the central meaning and we change the dance. Remain present and new dance steps appear. In actuality, everything is changing all the time, only stale patterns prevent us from seeing this truth. Let us be so bold as to hold onto nothing and see what materializes.

The practice is simple, not easy, but rewarding on many levels. As individuals and as the whole, we commit to consciously engaging with our organizations, associations, communities and as citizens of the world. We stand up and declare our intentions to be mindfully aware to all who will listen. As we do, moments when we are not present become more obvious and once seen, offer us another chance to choose the present moment of now and all it has to offer — insights, fresh perspective and connection.

Being Present to New Meaning

1.   For a moment, let go of believing that you have the answers. What does it feel like to not know? Comfortable? Difficult? Uneasy? Agonizing?

2.   What is your organization's contribution to the whole?

3.   What is the driving force — the meaning at the foundation of the workplace?

4.   What might incite passionate belonging and fuel success that you could position at the organization's core?

5.   Would the driving force be compelling for all four generations, as well as the diverse cultures within the organization?

6.   What social contract within the organization would demonstrate commitment? In other words, who will you be while you are doing your work?

7.   What would it mean to live and work with present moment awareness?

8.   Using present moment awareness, what old behaviors and activities would no longer be required?

9.   Which of your policies are based upon past failures?

10.   What would commitment to present moment thinking mean to performance reviews, ranking and rating, your vision, mission and values?

11.   What possibilities could present moment thinking inspire?

Chapter 7

Expanded Listening

The problems that exist in the world today cannot be solved by the level of thinking that created them.

— Albert Einstein

Stopping the Chatter; Opening Channels

Listening is easier when the mental chatter begins to subside. A quieter mind is a rewarding side effect of a present moment practice. We all get glimpses of great ideas and new solutions to old problems. Normally, we don't slow down long enough to recognize them. At times an idea comes through and we act upon it. Sometimes the idea comes through yet, we don't act, especially when it seems crazy or we don't quite understand the message. On occasion we know we've missed something special, even though we can't quite put our finger on it. A flow of inspiration and information is available to us all as the chatter dies down. The quieter our minds become — the fewer fears and limiting beliefs — the greater the flow of ideas. The stillness makes it easier for us to recognize the ideas before they evaporate.

The problems our workplaces and our world face today will exact a high price from us for their solutions. We created them when we were not consciously aware. We were under the influence of our short-comings and focused on not recreating the past. Or, we were trying to reconstruct the past, worrying that our future would not live up to yesterday's success. Whether we were trying to bring the past forward or leave it behind, both attempts were based on the past.

Anxiety creates solutions based in fear. We worry about tight credit, decreasing sales, escalating costs, what our competitors are up to, the commitment of our teams, and whether we are up to the task. Sometimes the worry is conscious, other times it is not. We are concerned about the impact on our profits and job security. We wonder what it all means to our future comfort and our plans for retirement. This worry and concern strangles our ability to respond in new and creative ways. We choke off the flow of ideas and stress our selves and the systems intended to support us. Without intending to, the focus becomes fear rather than possibility. Whatever we focus on determines the solution. From fear, we will always work to limit our losses rather than thinking big.

In today's world it is difficult not to be buffeted about by fear. Job losses and bankruptcy plague Circuit City, Dow Chemical, Rio Tinto, Sony, Linens 'n Things, Deutsche Post AG, Mervyns, 3M, Viacom, DuPont, AT&T, Credit Suisse, Pepsi, Citigroup, DHL — all big names. Globally we are waiting for the last shoe to drop and hoping there aren't many more shoes to come.

Organizations and individuals are struggling as they find themselves without a vision for their future, unable to see beyond today. It is as if we were speeding along comfortably at 80-miles-an-hour, our bright and shiny destination in sight, but hit a brick wall. Now everywhere we look, rather than finding proof that we can still reach our destination, we find dead-ends and detours. The future we had envisioned is gone. Waiting for it to re-emerge keeps us mired in the past. For many of us, it is difficult to imagine what is next, and especially tricky to picture how it will turn out well. Because of this, we are unintentionally sitting right in the middle of not knowing. And, it seems like the only thing we know for sure is that not knowing what's next isn't comfortable.

Clarity, and a degree of comfort, comes when we shift our framework from unintentional to intentional. The discomfort eases when we are willing to not know. Giving up on frantic speculation gives us a sense of peace and allows us to settle in to our new reality. As a result, we can set down the files filled with what has worked and what hasn't worked before. This clarity comes when we stop believing we know what is possible. Our willingness to listen without knowing opens channels of information that help us move forward. The information shows us the way past the detours and dead-ends. It instills faith and purpose into what moments before felt empty and meaningless. Such faith is capable of rewiring everything we have believed to be true.

Scientists, artists and writers have encountered this sacred place of not knowing. We enter into it consciously or unconsciously, right before a breakthrough. For me, the magnitude of the breakthrough is generally mirrored by the extent of my agitation just before I let go of old programs. The greater my attachment to a particular belief, the more difficult it is to release, the more powerful the insights that follow. It makes sense — the larger the belief that falls away, the greater the space for new wisdom. We all have experienced this sacred place — times when we disappeared into the flow or when we were filled with awe by a sunset or the face of our newborn child. The key is to enter into it intentionally — and we do with practice.

In yesterday's world, sitting silently in our offices or cubicles, and listening for solutions, would have been seen as a bit eccentric and unproductive. In the new, consciously evolving world, quiet spaces will support individuals and groups looking for emergent answers. We will come together, enter intentionally into not knowing, and open the space for new questions and new solutions. We will consciously create information-rich moments of insight.

The spiritually aware work of MIT's Peter Senge, Jon Kabat-Zinn's mind-body workshops for corporate executives, and vipassana teacher, Mirabai Bush's work with corporations like biotech giant Monsanto all point to new acceptance of a deeper listening. Bush's Center for Contemplative Mind in Society coordinates programs on 75 college campuses that incorporate contemplation into professions from architecture to science — and even includes a program at West Point Military Academy. [16]

Business people across the world are listening. Embracing meditation, taking time each day to sit in silence and center ourselves isn't just for monks any more. In fact, it is a vital part of not just surviving, but thriving in these uncommon times. Senior executives are listening for ideas and insights, and opening new, burgeoning channels of receptivity. Evolving organizations are willing to use all the tools available to them, knowing that only a previous lack of understanding caused them to see skepticism instead of promise in evolutionary ideas.

Energy Awareness

A fundamental aspect of listening is energy-based. We each understand more about energy than we realize. Energy isn't some out-there concept. We are always aware of it, even though not always consciously. When we walk into a room we automatically feel the energy. We know instantly if the room is hostile without a word being said. We also know if the energy is dead flat or welcoming.

It's common to talk about listening styles, body language and tone — the intangibles of communication — but not as common to talk about energy and its impact on listening and communication as a whole. Energy, once a taboo like the *softer* people skills used to be, is no longer unmentionable. Some business people still resist learning about both aspects of communication, but not talking about energy, when so many people can grasp its presence is downright silly, not to mention perilously unproductive. This is especially true once we begin to realize the powerful potential that an appreciation of energy has for creating authentic communication.

In the years to come, everyone will be talking about energy, its impact on our ability to listen deeply, and how it helps us to connect the dots of our communication puzzles and achieve new levels of understanding. Evolving organizations are always ahead of the curve and they will pave the way by experimenting and learning to capitalize on energy.

The benefit to organizations is extensive. As we learn to recognize our personal energy patterns, we are able to monitor our own energy during conversations. It is easier to recognize when we are projecting our personal concerns into the words of another. In simple terms, we are more self-aware. Clearer awareness helps us understand that interpretation is a personal event happening within the confines of our heads alone. We choose how we interpret another's words or events. This self-awareness is the beginning point of personal responsibility.

As we practice, we are able to see how our energy impacts others and our ability, or inability, to connect. Being able to sense energy allows each of us to ask appropriate questions and understand what is really happening. For example, if we are talking with someone and sense disconnection or an unwillingness to listen — a skill that is attainable for all of us — we can stop and ask about what just happened. In the process we can learn what people are afraid to say. This information is invaluable and is lost without energy awareness. We can also sense when someone deflates the room's energy with judgment, blame or resignation, and play our parts in ending inappropriate miscommunication or damaging behavior.

Another benefit of studying energy awareness is that the education fine tunes our bodies. They become more capable of telling us when we are on to something pure and true, and when we are chasing old shadows of belief, and limiting ourselves with outdated solutions. Once we know how to check ourselves, and our new ideas, using techniques like meditation, visualization, and applied kinesiology, we add a new tool to our evolutionary toolbox that will help us move forward on a straighter, therefore faster, path towards success.

In today's workplace health care costs are skyrocketing. Energy recognition is a tool that helps to alleviate stress. Once we notice energetically, that we are headed into negativity, we can address it. Couple energy awareness with meditation and there is significant proof of its success. Statistics coming out of Jon Kabat-Zinn's meditation courses are undeniable.

> "Overall, controlled clinical studies carried out by the center have documented symptom reductions of between 29 percent and 46 percent among class participants. Breaking it down by condition, people with heart disease experienced a 45 percent reduction in symptoms; high blood pressure, 43 percent; pain, 25 percent, and stress, 31 percent. Those are the kind of numbers that get the attention of health care providers trying to control costs. Insurance companies and HMOs like Tufts are now picking up at least some of the cost for about a quarter of the program's participants."[17]

Try it yourself and notice the difference in your physical, mental and emotional energy and you won't need further proof. Through awareness we learn to spot things that drain our energy and leave us tired and wasted at day's end. We can all learn to sense what energizes us and others and create nurturing workplaces that foster the health and wellness of all players.

Once we know what depletes us and what rejuvenates us, we are far more likely to take personal responsibility and make choices that benefit ourselves and our workplaces. The benefit to the individual is a new, energized sense of potential that translates into engaged and willing employees for the organization.

A side effect of being proficient at energy awareness is that we see the thoughts, beliefs or ideas that close us down more quickly. This is easily experienced with an experiment. Say the word *yes* and play with how it feels in your body. Say it again and listen carefully. Now, say the word *no* and feel it in your body. Say it slowly and pay attention. *Yes* opens us energetically; *no* closes us down. Yes correlates with acceptance or love. No correlates with rejection or fear. No is in essence saying *not this*. When we feel closed down our bodies are telling us we are in resistance, that we are rejecting what is present. Our bodies teach us to be present and experience whatever is happening directly. The purpose of the tightness is to help us become skilled at discerning the underlying message. The message isn't to close down or to run and hide. It is saying, "Take a look. What in this moment do you disagree with? What can't you accept as reality or as a possibility? Why aren't you present?"

All day long we are either in acceptance or resistance to what is going on around us — an aspect of our work, the people we work with, the quality of our interactions, or our dependence on people or other departments within the business. If we are honest, most of the time, we are in resistance. Resistance doesn't help us make good decisions, but stopping and paying attention — returning to the present moment — makes good decisions possible. As we unclench from resistance — which is attachment to our answer — it is simply common sense that more options are available since resistance prevents any new answer from emerging.

Acceptance of *now* is the starting place, not the ending place. First we accept *what is* and from that place we see what there is to do next. Our action is based upon the true reality, rather than on our fears about an imaginary reality when we start with acceptance. This new energy awareness is a powerful tool to help us make sense of our world. With it we automatically come back to the present moment — to what is actually here, right now. Once present, we can listen to all voices, including the intuitive voice of wisdom and clear direction.

It is common to question the answers we receive when we are new to expanded listening. So, how does one know if the answer is accurate or just the product of old mental programs? Solutions from the universal knowledge bank never harm our world. They are aligned with mutual gain. Often they are quite surprising, a total right turn from what we expect. They appear only when we settle into not knowing the answer, when we are willing to listen for a more complete and perfect resolution. The solutions often stretch our understanding in new ways and require us to share our understanding with others, who in turn, add their understanding to the complexity and create a more complete answer.

If we are hunting inside our minds, worrying or fearful about receiving an answer, what we hear will be fearful. If we are looking for a solution to appease our ego and make us feel good, the answer will be created out of a sense of need — out of lack. When we are focused on protecting our self the answer will be limited. If we pretend to be present in order to receive an answer, the answer will be incomplete and cause unforeseen disconnects down the road.

For years the timber products industry clear-cut the forests. They didn't think to replant. They were in the business of getting the logs out of the woods to make lumber. It was the way the entire industry worked. At the time, it appeared to be a win for the company and for the workers. They made a decent living and the consumers had materials to build homes and businesses. It wasn't until much later that decision-makers recognized the need for replanting. Sustainable woodlands meant jobs for our children and grandchildren, recreational opportunities for everyone, renewed wildlife habitat, and more trees meant beautiful forests and more oxygen for the planet. We didn't notice that our decisions were short-sighted, that we had missed part of a much bigger picture. If we had been present and practicing our expanded listening skills we would have.

Listening energetically is an art. As with all works of art, it takes time to paint a masterpiece. Leonardo daVinci didn't paint *The Last Supper* in an hour. Learning to use the full potential of conscious listening is a gradual process too. The practice is simple yet can take a lifetime to perfect. Stop and pay attention to your thoughts. Listening begins as simple thought awareness. Stay present to whatever appears. The mental chatter of thoughts will slow down. When it does, ask your question if you have one and settle in and be willing to wait for an answer. It may not come during your practice, so be patient. Be open to the answer materializing when you least expect it. Observe any impulse you have to speed up the process and short-cut the answer. Your answer, when it comes, will be filled with the energy of yes. The more you practice listening consciously the easier it will be to recognize the answer.

Eventually our organizations will be able to check energy threads and see whether a particular idea is timed and pollinated sufficiently to blossom. Listening carefully we will hear yes, no, or not now...wait a bit, or do this first and check back. Imagine what we will create when we don't waste time and resources spinning our wheels in unproductive effort? Think what good we will do in our world with real-time inside information.

From the small idea or project, to world-wide implementations, expanded listening can shorten time durations, lessen resource requirements, add meaning for employees, and keep us from unintended consequences. Whether we believe in it or not, isn't that kind of payoff worth taking a chance on, even if we end up looking foolish? What is the worst that could happen—a drop in blood pressure and a return to sleeping like a baby? Even the less enlightened can see that's a pretty good downside.

Listening Consciously

1.   Do you have a vision? How has it, or your belief in it, changed in the last year?

2.   To what degree are you aware of your thoughts? Does your mind chatter annoy you or do you view it as an opportunity to see what's there?

3.   Have you attempted to slow the mind chatter and listen to your subconscious beliefs and thoughts? If so, what have you tried that worked well…and why?

4.   How successful were you? Were you surprised by anything you heard?

5.   Are you energetically aware? Can you sense when energy is flat or blocked?

6.   What is your normal response when you sense uninviting energy?

7.   What drains energy from a room, the organization, you personally? What energizes?

8.   Have you trusted or dismissed your intuition in the past? What was the result?

9.   What benefit could you or your workplace derive from trusting inner knowing and insight?

Chapter 8

Let's Play

A childlike man is not a man whose development has been arrested; on the contrary, he is a man who has given himself a chance of continuing to develop long after most adults have muffled themselves in the cocoon of middle-aged habit and convention.

— Aldous Huxley

A New View of Work

What would happen if we called it *play* instead of *work?* Does work have to be serious in order to be responsible? Are the ideas of fun and work incompatible? Is it possible for work to be amusing, to be recreation? An enlightened mind — and each of us has at least a sliver of mind in that category — would say, "Yes, work can be play, or… it seems it could be."

Think about the last time you walked into an office and heard laughter. What was your first thought? Was your automatic conclusion that people were working or messing around? Most likely, you thought the great American (substitute your country of origin) work ethic had been abandoned. Why is that? When did we decide that work had to be work — that it had to be such serious stuff?

There are many reasons that work devolved into serious business, all of which circle back to our acceptance of the seven workplace myths as fact rather than fiction. Understanding the myths and learning to appreciate a different reality allows us to embrace the idea of work as play.

FIRST—The World Is a Scary Place

The first myth, *The World Is a Scary Place,* sets the tone, doesn't it? Here is how it goes. Bad things happen. Obviously it is important to keep bad things from happening to us, so be on the look-out for (read that as focus on) bad things.

Belief in this basic myth sets more than a tone of dread, it also sets up our negative interpretations — all the ways we spin events inside our personal and organizational stories. It creates winners and losers, and induces us to protect ourselves. If this was not a scary world, there wouldn't be a need to protect and defend our ideas and beliefs, our status and possessions, or our loved ones, ourselves included. We would care about each other's success because we wouldn't be as concerned about our own. The myth sets up the ongoing battle of the fittest where only the strong have a right to survive. It keeps us in line with terms like fight the good fight, earn your stripes, bite the bullet, take one for the team, and get on board or get run over.

Fear is not, nor has it ever been a motivator. It may stimulate a reaction, but it does not motivate. It cannot inspire a whole response. In Anwar Sadat's famous words:

> "Fear is, I believe, a most effective tool in destroying the soul
> of an individual — and the soul of a people."

Fear is a restraining device, like a spider's thread. It sticks to us and keeps us from moving forward or seeing clearly, wrapping us in the web of self-protection. Fear either turns us into a cubicle rat waiting for more bad news and sinking deeper into doom, or triggers a fight or flight response. None of these options benefit the individual or the organization, nor should they be acceptable; they prevent us from being present.

> It is a vicious circle. Our fears make us skeptical. The skepticism leads to a lack of trust. Without trust we fear fully connecting with others...The degree to which we hold back or withhold emotions, feelings, or communication because of the fear, is the degree to which fear has a grip on us and can therefore determine our behavior. We are enslaved and limited by the need to hide what is really going on with us because we aren't sure whom we can trust. The belief in a scary world is entwined around our physical, mental and emotional security - — or lack there of. It creates the need to always be thinking about how to protect and defend ourselves. — The Grand Experiment [18]

The alternative to the first myth adds a little room for play. The world isn't a scary place; it just is. We give it meaning by the way we interpret what happens and by the decisions we make. We are always in control of our response and our response determines our outcome. If we are closed to options and looking for the downside we will find it; that is a certainty. If we are willing to see everything as opportunity, at the least as opportunity for growth, we will see things we couldn't see with our eyes closed.

Seeing our world as a playground, as a mystery unraveling before our eyes, turns everything that happens, even apparently negative outcomes, into data points brimming with information. Fear doesn't stop us. Our thoughts about fear stop us. Fear is merely a picture inside our heads about something we do not want to take place, something that, if we investigated, would fall apart. Is the world a scary place? We each decide. With our decisions we determine the extent of our ability to respond and to take decisive action. When we let the fear stop us, it determines our world and paints it a fearful color, precluding us from making work into play. But, when we choose to see fear for what it is, creative energy in need of a little loving direction, we cross a threshold into a state of free will that actually is free. From that moment on we choose what we create, able to see the true issues that exist.

SECOND—There Is Not Enough

The second myth states, *There Is Not Enough*. This myth is all about lack. It is based in the belief that there aren't enough resources. In short, there isn't enough time, money, labor or materials for each of us to live a happy, prosperous life. Tie the second myth to the first and they ensure conflict, guaranteeing that some of us won't have what we need to live well, and that many of us will not have what we need to live at all.

Taking *not enough* to be factual makes people act in ways that confirm shortage. The actions unravel a self-fulfilling prophecy. Beliefs lead us to ideas and proof that reinforce the original belief. We see what we believe. Years ago scientists realized we don't see results contradictory to our beliefs, and created double and triple blind testing to counteract the belief-effect. Dr. Jeremy Wolfe, a Harvard ophthalmology professor, was asked about this effect in a CBS interview.[19]

"So, if you're not expecting it, or you know that it almost never happens, you're not likely to see it?" His response was enlightening. "Yes. The one liner is, if you don't see it often, you often don't see it."

Wolfe was referencing a 2006 test of Homeland Security baggage screeners in Chicago and Los Angeles. At O'Hare 60 percent of the time the screeners missed the fake bomb materials. In Los Angeles the numbers were worse. They missed the fake bombs 75 percent of the time.

The screeners don't expect to see the bombs, so they don't. As long as we give our faith to the second myth instead of clearing out the false so we can see what is true, we are fated to see what we expect as well, and go no further. In the workplace, this type of thinking feels like *work* in its most literal sense, and severely limits creative thinking and innovative problem solving.

A substitute to the second myth exists both as a possibility and as a leap of faith. Choosing to embrace *profusion* thinking amidst what appears to be definitive proof to the contrary, is actually our only chance at change. We won't know if there is enough until we take the leap and believe in its possibility. Only then, by the decisions we make and the actions we take will we be able to see the results of this new thinking. Accepting that the potential of abundance exists — that our world is a profusion of possibility — charts a new course. This new direction embraces the potential and erases our faith in lack's existence — the basic rationale for greed — taking with it many of the barren effects of our current society.

In 1994 Paul Lindenberg, a South African owner of a fast growing furniture company, found himself questioning why he had founded the company in the first place. Immense volatility surrounded the birth of South Africa's new government. It was a time of great intimidation and rampant fear. In the midst of the struggle Paul faced extremely high tool and equipment maintenance costs, an uninspired and entitled workforce, and a growing problem with quality. Some would have called his problems insurmountable.

Paul could see that a lack of accountability and quality controls were his prime flaws but there were no tools readily available to help him further analyze and turn his business around. He needed a plan for success. So, in the absence of a solution, he decided to develop one that encompassed all the variables and provided flexibility, adaptability, accuracy, and measurability. He reasoned that this new level of control would give him the accountability he needed to achieve his goals.

He didn't know it at the time, but he was acting from a belief that anything was possible. He believed he could create the missing resources. He didn't focus on the lack or the cards stacked against him. He saw possibility.

A few short weeks after Paul completed and implemented his ideas he saw clear indications that his business was headed in the right direction again. The staff became results-oriented. Those who were not contributing in a positive way were pressured by their co-workers to resign, decreasing their numbers by 20 percent. Despite a smaller workforce, productivity increased by one-third. Quality, efficiency, and equipment maintenance also improved dramatically. The workers became involved in the problem-solving process by recognizing where and how improvements and adjustments needed to be made. Tardiness and absenteeism dropped as people became fully accountable for their actions, workmanship, and performance. Due to the simplicity of the *point* system in his WayPointer Methodology, everyone could relate to performance indicators in a meaningful way. In Paul's words, "We all worked as a team with clearly defined objectives. The employees recognized that any problem or setback to the business would inevitably have an impact on themselves. Enthusiasm returned to the workplace and ultimately extended beyond in terms of customer satisfaction and reputation."

How different, not to mention how much more fun, could boardroom discussions be when we choose to believe solutions exist to every challenge, solutions that honor all — our employees and customers, vendors and competitors, our profitability and the well-being of our world? A bright future awaits us when we apply the same thinking to humanity's largest problems: poverty, illness, intolerance, terrorism, climate change, and access to education. Shifting our thinking from impossibility to the excitement of seeing these problems resolved in our lifetimes, or better yet, the near future, drives the innovation that will solve them. Our visions are too small. Let us paint a vision so big that all it can do is inspire, and see where we go from there? We choose what is possible. All that is required is a decision to move beyond small, sterile thinking and choose big.

THIRD—The Power Is Outside of Us

The Power Is Outside of Us parades as the third myth. Without this myth the victim disappears and everyone becomes part of the answer. This is not a myth that *others* believe and act within, even though most people would not consciously define themselves as a victim. Until the myth is investigated thoroughly, it is almost certain that each of us is under the influence of myth number three.

If we've ever cursed another in traffic — out loud, under our breath, or even with a tightening of our body — or blamed the organization or government for a decision or outcome, we are a casualty of victimhood. If we've criticized the economy, regulations, and right or left wing politics, we are playing the role of victim. When we react to income taxes, our parents or our children, or wish the sun was shining when it rained, we are victims. Victims desire approval that didn't come and break promises to themselves and others for reasons they didn't foresee. The list is infinitely long and keeps the victim mentality alive and well. It is the natural outcome of ordinary human conditioning.

We generally do not choose to see ourselves as victims. It sounds bad and causes an immediate and automatic recoil action. Victimhood sets in the minute we buy into the idea that we are not in complete and absolute control. If we've ever set eyes on a newspaper, or listened to the evening news, we know control is illusive.

This myth is tricky. Most of us are not 100 percent victims 100 percent of the time. Our inner victim comes and goes, making it more difficult to pin down. Often it arrives in tandem with something we take to be factual, something that supports our right to feel powerless. We see it as truth, not victimhood.

In the workplace the myth is easy to spot in others. But, as we become astute observers, we also begin to see the myth-in-action in our own lives. It is always present when we hear a complaint. It accompanies the grouch as surely as it does the disillusioned. It is a chief cause of employee disengagement and lost productivity. Like a corrosive acid, it eats away at overall organizational and human success.

Watching for the victim in others gives us a closer look into our patterns and helps us identify our own reactions. As we watch, if we are open to seeing the ways in which we too are victims, we gain understanding of our personal triggers. We are also able to amend the decisions we have made about our ability to be effective and to make a difference.

Admitting that we are being a victim is tough to swallow. Our egos resist in-depth scrutiny. However, refusing to consider the like-lihood guarantees that we remain victims. It is a great personal and organizational disservice to refuse to explore one's inner realms and to see the inside stories that are making the decisions and deter-mining what is possible.

Once we decide to experiment and see what's in charge of our beliefs and behaviors, an alternative path emerges. With the third myth that path creates an opening for personal responsibility. This requires a choice. But, since we have clearly seen the victim within, making the choice is far easier. Realizing that we are — and always have been — making decisions that empower or victimize us, the only enlightened option is choosing empowerment. Who would consciously choose to remain a victim when they could play with others and realize a greater potential?

Seeing through the lens of powerlessness, we couldn't see the potential. We were so serious, a clear sign of self-protection, that we cut ourselves off from our natural curiosity. From the new vision, instead of waiting to be told what to do, and when to do it, we drive our own personal accountability. We see that our happiness and success depend on our own actions. Rather than holding our organ-izations hostage, making them responsible for our job satisfaction, we see that with every choice and every interpretation we make, job contentment is entirely our responsibility. We become the effect of our choices, rather than being at the effect of others. And, that trans-lates into a personal stake in success.

FOURTH—*We Are Not Enough*

We Are Not Enough is the fourth myth. It doesn't matter how many individuals we work with, from the CEO through brand new hires, myth four is always present. It shows up as arrogance and shyness, perfectionism and self-doubt. It stops many good ideas, and even greater people, before they break through the sound barrier. It prevents as many ideas and solutions from being heard, as it does the initial insight from being spoken.

Until we are willing to do the challenging work, we are at the effect of number four. Even those of us who believe we have managed to skip this one, either through luck or good genes, when brave enough to look, will find more than a trace of proof that the myth lives on.

Productive ground to explore is our degree of flexibility, our ability to completely trust others and ourselves, our judgments both subtle and overt, and the fearlessness with which we engage. Our reactions to other's opinions, the level of our compassion, and the times when just being our ordinary, everyday self doesn't quite seem enough have potential as well. These inner places are rich with information. Once the surface layers are cleared, many other carefully hidden sites are exposed.

To dismantle the fourth myth it is important to make friends with the psychological concept of projection. In basic terms, projection is a defense mechanism through which we assign our personal traits and unacceptable or unwanted thoughts, behaviors and emotions to someone else. From the standpoint of projection, any judgment we make about someone should be questioned. This is easier to accept as soon as we realize that every thought, emotion and judgment takes place within our mind and is filtered through our programming. Humans constantly determine the value and meaning of everything, choosing from an infinite number of explanations. We can see this with the diversity of opinions in our world, many of which are at odds. We choose the interpretation that fits our experiences — our encoded programming.

As we walk past our co-worker's office we hear laughter and quiet voices. Whether we stop or not, our interpretation of what just occurred will depend on what we believe about ourselves. It is common to make assumptions, believing our peers were talking about us or hiding something. The judgment is actually self-judgment; it is about us and is based upon our sense of worth at the time. Assumptions, the natural outcome of projection, damage relationships and our ability to work together to get things done. A revealing question to ask is, "Out of all the interpretations available to me, why did I choose that one?"

Projection, those thoughts and motivations we assign to another, when used to point out our beliefs — our personal brainwashing — shows us our slant on life and our inclinations about ourselves. Getting a good look can stop our skewed viewpoint from tilting the world in ways that create more fear and doubt. Feeling good about our lives doesn't need to take a lot of effort. When we aren't untangling ourselves from not being enough we have the energy and inclination to extend our viewpoint beyond ourselves. As long as we unwittingly burden ourselves with self-protection, we make small decisions. Breaking loose from our small viewpoint, we automatically look for, and find solutions, that serve a larger purpose and audience.

As individuals and their organizations see the way they think and play small, they grow into personally responsible people, and capable, cohesive teams, who think big and take the actions necessary to realize their dreams. Literally anything is possible for an organization not hamstrung by the fourth myth.

For the organization the benefit of dismantling the *not-enough* myth appears obvious, but there is a side benefit that increases the payoff tenfold. When we are willing to see ourselves as enough, we automatically begin to see others as enough as well. Countless studies have shown that how we view another determines how they show up. When we see their potential, people rise to new heights of performance. This myth has a domino effect. It only takes one person to see through the myth, and a replicative effect spreads throughout the entire organization, eventually making it enough too — capable and able of generating constant miracles of success.

FIFTH—There Is One Right Way

Turf wars, idea assassins, change paralysis, micro-management, tunnel vision and short-sightedness are all signs of the fifth myth, *There Is One Right Way*. Any one of these, let alone all, kills an organization's heart, soul and ability to survive long-term. *One Right Way* is not just the way we consciously do things. It includes every way we think within any box, conscious or not.

Individuals have right ways as do organizations. For individuals the one right way includes everything from how we think life should be to our personal rationale for not changing. It also contains how we believe others should behave, our unquestioned beliefs — those things we don't dare challenge — and every other box, big or small into which we sandwich ourselves and our world.

The list is exponentially longer for the organization. It incorporates all the individual boxes, and the bigger, collective boxes intended to circumvent exceptions to rules and give us standards of measurement. It contains our vision, the strategy and ways to execute the plan. As if that weren't enough, it also includes the unintended boxes that won't give up the ghost, even though we quit focusing on them long ago. Somewhere, someone who missed the memo sits besides a file cabinet guarding a specific right way that long ago turned wrong.

When we combine the right ways of individuals with the right ways of the organization it's a wonder that anything new and innovative is ever conceived, let alone brought into form. Right ways are responsible for individual rigidity and the resulting resistance or apathy towards new ideas — something every organization must overcome if they intend to be in business tomorrow. The depth and breadth of vision, tactics and structures, momentum and adaptability, all suffer as a result of right ways.

The fifth myth is easy to spot. Anytime *should* is spoken, a right way is close by. As the search for the right ways starts in earnest, and we move beyond customary *right* thinking, it is feasible to accept that anything we say *no* to is also a right way.

Right ways constrict and paralyze even when they appear to be based in fact. They prevent us from dreaming and playing the wonderful game of *what if*. When there is no right way to do anything, people are free to discover better and better ways to accomplish the impossible.

The search for all the right ways, when followed to its ultimate conclusion, brings an organization into the present moment, with myriad possibilities to explore. The antidote to the *right way* is the *many ways*. There are countless ways, none right and none wrong. All are filled with potential. With an unlimited focus, we move beyond the small claim we staked out in our adherence to rightness, and are able to access boundless growth.

SIXTH—We Know What Is Real

The sixth myth, *We Know What Is Real,* at first glance appears to be the same as *The One Right Way* because it too is based on knowing. Where as the right way is based in beliefs that show up in the physical — those things we can see, touch, taste, smell, feel and hear — *What Is Real* speaks to our relationship with our sixth sense, what some call intuition.

Many years ago we relegated intuition to the janitor's closet, at least as far as business was concerned. The intuitive was demeaned, laughed at, and scorned to such a degree that most of us quit acknowledging our intuition, even though we still sporadically caught glimpses of it. A heightened sense of self-protection made us keenly aware that reality was what everyone else accepted. It didn't matter if other's reality didn't match our personal experience. We learned to discount our knowing and reinforced our belief that we weren't enough in the process.

The large problem with this thinking is that as long as we are committed to what we think we know to be true, we are limited to what we think we know. It sounds like a riddle or circular logic, but it isn't as innocuous as a mental game. The known can never get us to the unknown, to that place where innovation resides. This is no different than standing with our feet firmly planted on the ground while attempting to fly.

It wasn't too long ago that our world was flat and the Earth was the center of the universe. At one time both were scientific facts. It is apparent, even to the casual observer, that reality shifts and changes as we expand our ability to understand and discern. It took a courageous man taking the risk of falling off the edge of the world, and another being imprisoned for his heretical beliefs to prove differently.

The extent of our courage limits or enlarges our ability to fathom what is true. It takes courage to believe in a reality others can't see. Conformity is behind our reluctance to fully express ourselves and determines what we believe to be real, therefore shrinking our personal dreams and workplace visions. Courage is the anecdote for conformity. Once we understand that we alone give our worlds meaning, that abundant potential actually exists, that the power is in our own hands, and that we lack nothing, courage doesn't require something extraordinary. It isn't reserved for the special few. Courage, the audacity to know that we can and will make a difference, is as normal as breathing. And, when courage no longer prevents us from challenging accepted truths we will have made it a long way towards becoming fully functioning human beings.

SEVENTH—We Are Separate and Alone

We Are Separate and Alone is the last myth. It is the foundational myth for all the others, for if we didn't believe we were separate, the other myths would crumble. The conviction of our separateness feeds them all. The first six myths require the seventh for their existence, and the seventh creates the other six. This is circular. Truth does not need defending. When one is willing to see, it is obvious. Only a falsehood requires a defense.

Our disconnection allows us to find solutions that serve a tiny minority, without consideration for those who are diminished as the few are increased. This myth has a sting. If I am separate then I am not connected to you. What you do doesn't affect me. What I do does not affect you. We all know this is not true, but we still feel as if we don't belong. We feel isolated, distant from community. And, we feel a deep sense of loss.

With the recent events, it is more difficult to see ourselves, and our lives, as disconnected. The economy of the United States crumbled in 2008, and world economies fell as well. The financial well-being of each of us is perched precariously upon the whims of governments and institutions. Gas prices rose and our food prices followed. Farmers switched from growing food to eat, to growing grains for ethanol, and world starvation increased. In Australia, in order to save native seabirds, feral cats were removed from a famous Australian island and the rabbit population exploded, destroying much of the vegetation the seabirds required to survive.

If we open our eyes and minds we see the proof of our inter-connectedness. If some of us sicken the planet and she dies, where will the rest of us live? We live on a small round ball together. We breathe the same air; require the same soil and sunlight for our food and bodies. What any *you* does, impacts every *me*.

The myth is costly. For if we knew the truth that we are all connected, interdependent and inseparable, supportive of and supported by each other, would we be scared? Would we take from each other or feel powerless? Would we believe that we weren't enough or that our way was the only way? Wouldn't it be obvious that reality is expanding right along with our universe, and it's necessary to expand our awareness and comprehension to keep up? Wouldn't we be relentless creative forces for our own good, knowing our good included the good of all others? At the worst, choosing to see our connectivity is simply educated selfish-ness. At the best, it means a quickening of evolution, that we have taken the momentous step from *me* to the *ME* we were meant to be!

It's Always Celebration Time!

For a moment — or for the remainder of your life — picture your workplaces as communities with caring, worry-free individuals who are at last beyond fixation on the past and on the future, and are firmly planted in the present moment. What would that mean? If we were no longer measured by our past, regardless of whether it held failures or successes what would that imply? In fact, if we were not measured at all, and instead allowed to create and innovate based on our grandest vision, of what would we be capable? If we weren't worried about matching or exceeding past successes, or hindered by old tapes inside our heads reminding us of all the things that could and have gone wrong, what would we be willing to attempt?

Every day we choose what mountains to climb and conquer based upon the probability of success. What is possible is a moving target. Everest was an impossible challenge until Sir Edmund Hilary and Tenzing Norgay reached the summit in 1953. Another impossible event occurred in 1978. Messner and Habeler completed a successful ascent without supplemental oxygen, a feat no one had accomplished before. Many who watch the world of climbing admire oxygen-free summit attempts; others think them insane. Like all things, this is a question of beliefs.

If we reached the summit of poverty eradication, or any of our world's most serious challenges, it wouldn't matter if we used oxygen, or for that matter used any of the tools available to us. It would be time to celebrate. Every step we take forward into what was previously thought impossible, is a moment of grace for ourselves and our world. Grace, another word for unlimited possibility, is a step into the sacred. As we step forward, we walk on hallowed ground, untainted by our previously believed versions of possibility. It is timeless, effortless flow. It is discovery. It is a catalyst for exploration. It is play.

Moments such as these are cause for celebration, and every moment holds the potential of such grace. Whether we choose to enter into collaboration with possibility, and step off solid ground into the groundless determines the future of our organizations and of humanity. The time has passed for winning at all costs, unless the win is for us all. It is time to take the best from the past and improve upon it. C. A. Beard's words ring true nearly one hundred years after they first were spoken.

> "I am convinced that the world is not a mere bog in which men and women trample themselves and die. Something magnificent is taking place here amidst the cruelties and tragedies, and the supreme challenge to intelligence is that of making the noblest and best in our curious heritage prevail."

This is the choice with which we are faced. Every choice we make moves us closer to the noblest and best, or further away. It is actually a simple choice with broad implications. We can continue to make a life at the expense of others or learn to play together at last.

Celebrating Play

1. *The world is...you give it meaning* — What implication would this have on how you view yourself, others within the organization, or the organization as a whole? What are the implications for the competition, the customer, or the society in which life plays out?

2. *There is abundant potential* — If you believed this, how would your inter-departmental relationships, marketing and advertising planning, or budgeting change?

3. *The power is within* — No victims are allowed. How would the no victims rule change your organization and the lives of each individual within? What impact would full personal responsibility have on productivity, creativity, and employee relations?

4. *Everyone is enough — capable and able* — Were each member of the organization to integrate this possibility, what would that mean to individual or organizational potential? How much time and resources would you pick up if accountability was self-driven?

5. *There are many paths, many ways* — What would a focus on unlimited possibility mean to the organization and to the employees? What would a truly empowered workforce look like and of what would it be capable?

6. *We may not know what is real but we can discern reality with practice* — Imagine what it would feel like to put down the burden of having to have the answers. What could be gained in system and product innovation if everyone within the organization believed that anything was achievable?

7. *We are not separate and alone; we are in this together* — If we completely accepted our interdependence and interconnectivity with each other — all others — how would

decision-making change? What new and creative possibilities would we choose? How would our world change? What would belonging to a world that cared for each and every one of us mean personally and organizationally?

Chapter 9

Convening Minds and Hearts

We are no longer small, emotionally reactive human beings with problems and issues to solve. Instead we are becoming creational source beings who share a dance with Life, who seek the very best in ourselves and others, and who invent a new reality by loving it passionately and powerfully into being.

— Source Unknown

Stepping Clear of the Blind Zone into Shared Leadership

As long as we're in the organizational game, an appreciation of the evolving workplace and what is not only possible, but happening now, is fundamental to success. With this new knowledge we have the ability to reshape our organizations and their numerous connection points in the world and improve our capacity to thrive in these uncommon times.

Throughout the history of business, people have been bringing minds together to accomplish goals. Sometimes the goals aligned with the personal beliefs and values of those charged with implementing them; sometimes they didn't. Whether beliefs and values clashed or not wasn't given too much consideration. It was work, and doing things that didn't inspire us, or that clashed with our personal ethics, was expected. Trust in the leader — the more senior mind — was deemed critical to the organization's success. So, a culture of good followers was created. Career success often banked upon how well we followed.

Are good followers those who blindly follow, or are those who are willing to step up and lead as well, actually better followers? From a general's point of view, wouldn't it be important to know where the landmines are buried? If the troops knew, wouldn't it be nice if they said something before someone stepped right on top of one? For the leader, the challenge lies in determining who has the knowledge, who has the situation handled, and who, whether seemingly or actually, does not. This is especially troublesome, for both the troops and the general, if the general falls into the latter category.

There isn't a general or CEO out there who would consciously send his troops into a field of landmines, especially if there was a detailed map available. None of us is that knowingly arrogant, unless we are uncontrollably driven by our ego and have no concern for life. However we often believe we have the answers, that we are supposed to have the answers, or that it would show weakness to admit we don't. All of those beliefs are entrance points into the *blind zone*. As soon as we enter it, we set our toes, and those of our people, on top of a loaded landmine. If we stop and ask, or better yet, invent a culture of shared leadership that requires people to ask naive questions and share knowledge, we find that comprehensive drawings of the landmine locations exist.

Shouldn't the best leaders be capable of following as well as leading? Does it really matter who is the leader, or who is the follower if we are enormously successful? If it matters, we might want to go back to the basics and see which fears are in control of our common sense. If we refuse to evolve, we will be left behind.

Ricardo Semler the CEO and majority stockholder of Semco

International refuses to be the only leader. Twenty-five years ago he decentralized the family business that was previously a traditional Brazilian company. He has always been ahead of the curve. The new model he created encourages everyone to ask why and continually question if the way things are currently being done is still good for the company. He once said,

> "Semco's ongoing transformation is a product of a very simple business philosophy: give people the freedom to do what they want, and over the long haul their successes will outnumber their failures."

Semco doesn't control its managers either. At Semco, leadership has nothing to do with hierarchy. This democratic organization stripped away special treatment for managers including parking spaces and secretaries. Managers are anonymously evaluated every six months by their staff. If they don't measure up, they no longer fill the role of manager. Semco doesn't even prescribe what management courses to take; in fact, all employees are given a budget to manage their own development and training. Anyone who is interested can view the financials and there are courses to help them learn and understand the information. There are only six rules. 1) Forget about the top line. 2) Never stop being a start-up. 3) Don't be a nanny. 4) Let talent find its place. 5) Make decisions quickly and openly. And 6) Partner promiscuously.

With Ricardo Semler's radical form of participative management employees decide everything for themselves, including hours, managers, salaries, and training. To the traditional mind it sounds like heresy, but Semco's success is hard to argue with. There is about one percent turnover among the 5,000 employees. Revenue has grown 20 to 30 percent a year from four million in 1982 to more than $200 million in 2007. When interviewed about why more companies aren't decentralized like Semco, Ricardo Semler said that managers are afraid to lose power and control. He admits it has been a lengthy process for them as people's conditioning is strong. Their success is something to aspire to regardless of the difficulty today. Semco is one of Latin America's fastest growing companies.

Our world is gaining in complexity daily. No one person has all the answers. The complexity requires us to relinquish the reins and pull the wagon in unity, engaging not just the minds, but the hearts of the entire team. How much more rewarding, fulfilling, productive, let alone enjoyable, would that be? Can you visualize an organization where each person actually wanted to be there? What would it be like if the entire team couldn't wait to collaborate, create and innovate? How would it feel to be part of a workplace where people were excited to see and feel their impact on each other, the organization, the community and their world? We can move beyond visualization into actualization as Semco has proven.

The idea of being fully engaged isn't a wide-eyed dream. It is what we humans naturally are. We are always engaged, either in being of good use, or feeling outside of usefulness. People are basically the same. We all want happiness and freedom. We are built to connect with each other. It is quite simple. What I want, others want, even though we may go about it in different ways. In the workplace that means doing meaningful work — good work — with good people, for the good of us all. What we do matters. Who we choose to be makes a difference. No action is unimportant; no thought is without meaning. We each are a part of the much bigger picture — the community of mankind.

Belonging to a community is more than something we do after work; it is inherent to our basic essence. It is also what our work-places can be, a community of inspired individuals. When we shift our focus from controlling and managing behaviors, to creating community, a new code of conduct emerges. It's one that doesn't squeeze us out the rotating doors of our workspaces in order to find true connection. Organizations that figure this out will strike it rich with a fresh emphasis on restoring community.

We are more than the sum of our parts. Offering our heart and mind we claim a larger purpose and intent than we can with just our minds. And, in concert with others, we create a more perfect solution than we ever could alone. When we come together for the benefit of us all, we tap the force of creation. That force drives and champions us, leading us to ever higher goals, unafraid of failure, certain of our ability to succeed.

Heart-filled Minds

1. What moves you from self-protection and engages your heart?

2. When your heart is engaged how productive are you?

3. How do you feel or react when you are inspired?

4. How do you feel or react when you are coerced?

5. What makes a good follower? Does the definition change when you are the leader rather than the follower?

6. What makes a good leader? How does your definition change when you are the leader? The follower?

7. What would shared leadership, where everyone was both follower and leader, personally responsible on all levels, mean to the organization? How would productivity and the related financials change?

8. What does being an accepted and useful member of a community mean to you?

9. What are you willing to do for an organization where you feel a strong sense of belonging? How would that be different from what you are willing to do for an organization where you feel disconnected? What could you or the organization do to reconnect?

Chapter 10

Eight Enlightened Logics

It is easy to perform a good action, but not easy to acquire a settled habit of performing such actions.

— Aristotle

A Fusion of Possibility – Embracing Evolution

At an intuitive level we already know what our logic can now address. When looked at logically, without old beliefs in the way, we can see that embracing evolution is in our own, albeit enlightened, best interest. Unfortunately, taking one evolutionary action will not change age-old habits. As with any routine behavior, it takes a bit of perseverance to consciously evolve. The Eight Logics are the core messages, interspersed throughout this book, and they are a blueprint for organizations that desire to be on the leading edge of evolution. They are common sense lessons capable of breaking the spell of habit.

#1 — *Accepting That What Is, Is What Is*

To say yes, you have to sweat and roll up your sleeves and plunge both hands into life up to the elbows.

— Jean Anouilh

The fact that *what is, is what is* seems obvious when we slow down enough to look at it. This moment is unchangeable. Our desire for this moment to be something other than what it is, to be different, locks us into our dance with habit. We are always right in the middle of the moment called *now,* and kicking and fighting against it, will not change it one whit. To the contrary, accepting the contents of our present moment grants us entry into the flow of possibility, and plunges us into the fullness of life up to our elbows. This messy experience of life is sorely missed when we stand aloof inside our rigidity and resistance. Although, the disconnection that results often fuels a desire for meaning, so nothing, not even our resistance, is a waste.

We believe that if we accept this moment as it is, we lose something very important to us. It feels like giving up or giving in. It seems that if we accept what is, we will be forever denied something better. When we surrender our version of what should be, and give it back to the unfolding mystery in front of us, we can easily and clearly see our next steps. Acceptance does not mean passivity. That term does a great disservice to the truth. Acceptance is saying, "Yes! This is what is." It allows us to clearly see all the aspects presented, including what appears to our minds as chaotic and unacceptable. When we do this, we see things we didn't see when our minds were in denial. We see new potential that would have slipped by unnoticed had we not opened our minds and eyes. When we don't see all aspects of *what is* we automatically and instantly begin trying to change it to our way of thinking, to our version of what is right and best, before we see the available and very present potential.

A simple example is the reaction of individuals with a more traditional perspective to Generation Y — those born between the mid 1970's through 2000. Generation Y's non-traditional dress, preference for flexible work hours, high degree of social consciousness, life balance requirements, and need to express themselves creates a fairly large ripple in the smooth pond of conformity. Many in the workplace automatically look for ways to mold the younger ones into a *business mindset* or look to management to do it for them.

If we stopped trying to change them and accepted them for who they are right now, we could see they are important to our organization's evolution. Each generation embodies the next blueprint and offers us clues to our adaptability and ultimately, our longevity. If we understood this, we would seize the opportunity to ask them and ourselves some weighty questions. What do they possess that we don't have? Which of their beliefs are important to our future? How can we learn from them and share what we know in the process? What can they tell us about our customers and society as a whole?

If we were curious enough to ask these questions, we might discover that Generation Y professes to believe that anything is possible. According to an Oregon Public Broadcasting special that aired in 2008, one out of five believes he or she will be famous one day. If we see their vision as a window into expanded potential, rather than a glimpse at impossibility, we tap into their inner commitment to make a difference, to be a contributing force in our world. As we look with open eyes, we also find that the younger set has their fingers on the pulse of what's next in technology. When approached with respect and genuine interest, Generation Y provides creative insights into a significant segment of society and can teach us when we abstain from trying to change them. We can enter with them into the continuum, where everyone is both teacher and student.

Attempting to change *the present moment of now* is not only an unconscious step out of effortless flow, it is also a step into stress, discomfort and less than what is attainable. In the United States, more than half of the 550 million working days lost each year due to absenteeism are stress-related. In the United Kingdom, figures suggest that more than 40 million working days are lost each year due to stress-related disorders.[20] Alleviating stress is not just the nice thing to do; it is a sound business practice that has a direct impact on the bottom line. As we quit fighting against what is, and slip off the boxing gloves, shoulders loosen, and hearts and minds relax and open. Freed of stress, we are able to see and make the most of new opportunities.

#2 — *Curiosity That Questions Everything*

> *When nothing is sure, everything is possible.*
> — Margaret Drabble

Question everything — your assumptions, what you take for granted, your beliefs, what you believe possible, and especially what you think is impossible. That statement to a conventional organization may be a bit threatening. What would get done if everyone questioned everything? Nothing would be accomplished. The more conventional business model concentrates power, decision-making, idea generation, and all other key aspects of business life. The degree to which power is concentrated, and in the hands of a few important people, is the organization's degree of convention and correlated need for conformity. The intensity of our reaction to this paragraph's opening statement is a good measure of how we too, prefer conformity over more evolutionary behaviors. The higher our preference for controlled, concentrated power, the more likely we are a ghost of business past, content with the success we have enjoyed.

Letting the pendulum swing indiscriminately from one business model to the other is not the message or the intent of the Second Logic. A more conventional model may have its place within organizations. It is however worthwhile to explore with curiosity and openness, regardless of organizational type, to see what areas of control are simply confining, detrimental — not necessary at all — and are in fact, exhausting the organization's lifeblood. Question everything, every reason and justification for the maintenance of concentrated power. Releasing power is uncomfortable and those of us in power unconsciously limit ourselves and our organizations to retain our hold.

What would have happened if GM and Chrysler had instilled the Second Logic of curiosity? What questions would they have asked years before arriving in Washington, hats in hand, looking for a public handout? What sacred cows would they have sacrificed upon curiosity's altar? What answers to questions about the consumer, the oil industry, or the competition could have clarified their decision-making process, and helped them veer away from their fateful direction? Did employees, or people within the dealerships, know something that would have helped them? What prevented them from asking the questions and being willing to hear the answers? The conventional business model, designed to control and command, unwittingly stifles this type of inquiry and the resulting treasure of information.

Would they have seen Toyota coming, or at the least, acknowledged they had problems that old answers and old ways couldn't solve? Would they have looked at different numbers differently and learned to analyze through new glasses? In GM's case, the auto manufacturer continued to look at internal measures of quality and success rather than ever-changing consumer requirements and the new challenges presented by the competitive marketplace. A few lines from *Change or Die*[21] resonate strongly.

> "Even in the face of vast research to the contrary, Detroit for years has convinced itself of the notion, completely unsubstantiated, that its vehicles are every bit as good as those built by the import companies," wrote New York Times reporter Micheline Maynard in *The End of Detroit*. "In fact, this was the very claim made one morning in 2002 by General Motors vice chairman Bob Lutz when he declared GM's vehicles the equals of those built by Honda and Toyota. Yet, that afternoon, GM recalled 1.5 million mini-vans."

What creative and innovative force wasn't tapped? Perhaps if GM and Chrysler had installed curiosity along with cruise controls, they would have sensed the market was changing, and changed their basic competencies. They would have been able to offer consumers what they were looking for and finding at the competitors.

Curiosity takes us out of our self-importance and seriousness. It is a return to the innocence of childhood. When we step back, away from our labels and beliefs, our minds open. From that stance, the inexplicable happens. We see new ways to work together. We actually grasp how interconnected we are and understand what actions to take to create the most positive effect on tomorrow. It is basic to making effective decisions that are built to last.

#3 — Openness to See New Answers

The important thing is this: to be able at any moment to sacrifice what we are for what we could become.
— Charles Du Bos

Questioning everything makes it all visible. The very act of knowing closes us off from hearing anything new. We continue down old roads, doing old things, looking for new success. Openness is required to see new answers. Our world is moving so fast that organizations encumbered with information bottlenecks can no longer keep up, let alone get ahead. Information today is so vast that it is impossible to efficiently extract it using archaic methods. If it's not new right now, it's old. One person, or a small group of persons, cannot know it all. It is not just that there is no longer time to wait; it is that each of us holds more and more pieces of the solution. If we want the biggest possible answers we actually do need all the pieces and that means, like it or not, that we need each other.

The old model of command and control can not access the full puzzle. When we are curious, and open to seeing new answers and solutions, we gain entrée to the minds of the entire organization, community and global marketplace. An abundance of ideas is available when we see the organization's touch points, internal and external, as our information gold mine. Indescribable riches are buried beneath concentrated layers of centralization.

The people closest to the customer and the product have pieces of the larger puzzle, as does everyone within the organization. Surprisingly, the pieces aren't always what linear thinking might conclude. Combined, they piece together a whole picture. By looking at the composite, organizations can see the incompleteness of ideas and the probability of unplanned costs — in dollars and in reputation — while there is still time to make adjustments. If we are willing to admit that we can't have all the answers, that in fact more complete answers are available when we listen as an entire team, we have an extreme competitive edge. It's one that might just allow us to live long enough to evolve into a next generation workplace.

Like most companies, Group Mackenzie, a leading design firm in the Pacific Northwest, was hit by the recession of 2008. Their business, dependent on the building industry as it was, could have been devastated if not for the creative and opportunistic response from the management team. Their competitive edge — they are open to new ideas from new places. All are involved, from the principals to the newest administrative assistant, in generating business and providing client service. One idea that clicked was generated by an entry level planner from the firm. There was a vacant piece of property near her house that she thought Group Mackenzie should take a look at and see if they could find a solution to develop it into something special. Because they were listening and investigating leads, the integrated design team at Group Mackenzie discovered that the piece of property was owned by one of their clients. With a little creative brainstorming they suggested new uses for the property that resulted in additional work for the company. As Todd Johnson of Group Mackenzie said, "Most of our customers are still in business…they are just doing different things than they used to do when business was booming. We have to understand what they are doing and see how we can be of service. If we do that, we will continue to be successful."

Tomorrow's great leaders are learning to listen with respect to the chaotic whole, to see the entirety of what is offered, and translate it into organizational success. They are relieved to admit that they do not have the answers. They are aware that as they let go of knowing, answers and solutions can bubble to the organization's surface. When the answers come from receptivity and openness they feed and sustain the creative force growing within the team. The leaders of the future are learning to let go of the control buttons, and recognize that all individuals, including those previously marked as low-performing or unimportant, hold information vital to survival. As they do, they see people learn and grow, rising to link into, and transcend beyond this new potential.

#4 — *Giving Answers Time to Evolve*

> *The moment one definitely commits oneself, providence moves too. All sorts of things occur to help one that would never otherwise occurred. A whole stream of events issues from the decision, raising in one's favor all manner of unforeseen incidents and meetings and material assistance which no man could have dreamed would have come his way. Whatever you can do or dream you can, begin it. Boldness has genius, power and magic in it. Begin it now.*
> — Attributed to Goethe

An absence of commitment is both the individual's and organization's nemesis in learning to accept *what is* with curiosity and openness. In today's fast moving world, we expect our experiences to reciprocate in kind with lightening speed. The patience of commitment that allows answers sufficient time to evolve is a rare and emerging commodity. Such change will break long-standing patterns that we unknowingly built over time. Our structures of beliefs about reality were patiently constructed. It is now up to us to remain consciously aware and patiently deconstruct our limiting actions, giving answers time to surface and develop. When we learn to good-naturedly await each piece of the picture as it snaps into place, we won't be as likely to jump to conclusions before we see the whole image.

If we slow down we actually speed up. It's a counter-logical leap. A desire for accelerated change moves us out of present moment acceptance into resistance, and actually slows us down, stopping up the flow of information. It is easy to understand when you think about how tensing up slows the flow of breath. Resistance is the same. It constricts the flow of information, energy, and participation. When we feel intimidated or perceive a lack of respect from others or our self, the natural response is resistance, because accepting the message challenges our self-worth. In their book, *Perfect Breathing,* Al Lee and Don Campbell explain this observable fact.

"Unfortunately, our unconscious response to stressful situations is often just the opposite of what is in our best interest. Our primal response to fear and anger is either to hold our breath or to revert to the quick, shallow breathing associated with the fight-or-flight response. Instead of responding in a relaxed, focused, objective state where every system in our body is fully oxygenated, relaxed, and energized, we react in an emotional, oxygen-depleted state.

While martial arts such as karate teach fighting techniques and physical control, one of the hardest aspects to master is the ability to relax. Our natural instinct in "combat" situations is to tense up our body while our breathing defaults to the short shallow breathing associated with fight-or-flight. But martial arts teach us that by relaxing our muscles, and breathing slowly and deeply, we are able to achieve a state where we are intensely aware and able to react with more speed, power, and creativity than when we are in a tense, reactive, battle-ready fighting posture. Through breath awareness, we can discover a calm, relaxed, alert, creative, and powerful state that is subconsciously communicated to those around us rather than the emotion-filled message 'I'm ready to fight.' This immediately opens up a whole range of options and outcomes that may not have otherwise been available to us, which we can now pursue unencumbered by the restrictive chains of our reactive emotions."[22]

From a state of resistance answers and solutions have difficulty surfacing. Relaxing and giving answers time to evolve actually takes us deeper into acceptance of the present moment, in effect saying that *what is in this moment* is adequate right now. It initiates trust in our ability to receive bigger answers, and at the same time establishes constancy to our trust. It says we will remain right here, right now, firm in our commitment to a more complete answer.

What is possible when we integrate the Fourth Logic? What would it mean to the organization and our world? When we slow down long enough to see the entire picture, we are able to see the unintended consequences of our actions before we take action. When we have patience to let the answers evolve, we find bigger answers, make fewer mistakes, have less re-do, and squander fewer resources in the process. In these challenging and difficult times when we are all doing more with less and want to make what we do count, that sounds like a true gift. It is. If governments integrated the fourth logic rather than mobilizing the tools of war, where would we be now? How much richer would life be without the threat of imminent destruction? If the banking industry had done the same, perhaps they would have developed programs in service to our society rather than instituting and facilitating risky home loans that in the end harmed everyone. Every organization benefits from the Fourth Logic, even though it seems contrary to a drive for speed.

#5 — Great Self-Trust and Steadfastness in Using the First Four Logics

> *If you stand up and be counted, from time to time you may get yourself knocked down. But remember this: A man flattened by an opponent can get up again. A man flattened by conformity stays down for good.*
> — Thomas J. Watson, Jr.

The Fifth Logic is the support structure of the first four. What we know cannot accompany us into the evolutionary future. As long as we hang on to what we know, it will not only hold us back, it drags us back into what we have been. Looking for proof that The Eight Logics make sense reinforces dependence on what is known. Proof is a *known* commodity. It requires results from the past for its reasoning. Answers based upon what is known cannot be fresh and new.

The greater trust we place in others' potential and in our own, the easier it is to be steadfastly swept into the evolutionary tide — for trust acts as a guiding light — and propels us forward. The decisive question is "What do we believe about ourselves and about others?" We know that we are capable of being much more. This fact causes us to be disappointed in ourselves and those with whom we work and play. If we didn't believe in this potential, we would never be disappointed. We know that untapped potential exists. If we believe in this promise then the next question is, "Can our current workplace model unleash this potential?" So far it has not. Those who are making evolutionary strides are fashioning new models.

Rob Folsom of USA Fed, a non-profit, international credit union with more than 61,000 members worldwide and more than $700 million in assets, understood the need to unleash potential. Rob is the chief strategy officer and has been a member of the senior management team since Mary Cunningham, the new CEO, turned USA Fed on its head eight years ago. Mary naturally brought her beliefs with her when she took over USA Fed in 2001. She believes that you push to the lowest level where the work can possibly be done and that this is accomplished through a culture of learning. The 180-degree shift was a real shock to the previously top down, militaristic organization.

After the shock wore off and USA Fed admittedly, weeded out those who couldn't adapt to the new system, they implemented a new hiring strategy. In the process of bringing new enthusiastic people into the business, Rob realized there was a platform for the vice presidents' ideas, but none for the managers. As a result Rob created a two-tiered system with a committee to filter ideas that came from the ranks, and another to manage the implementation of the less complicated ideas and determine the viability of the more complex ones. The more complex ideas were assigned to selected managers who researched feasibility with teams of their choosing.

Projects generally took three months to complete and the platform has been more than three years in the making.

Last year kudos began rolling in. The platform did a great job of idea generation and the team it helped to create surpassed Rob's expectations. The team focused on measureable results and is getting things done. Rob says the most fun he has is championing other people's new ideas. There is a renewed sense of pride that has impacted the culture long-term. Those who knew USA Fed eight short years ago wouldn't recognize it now. With banks going under or struggling to stay afloat, USA Fed is experiencing positive growth.

I asked Rob about his biggest lessons. His candor was refreshing. With laughter as he poked fun at himself, he shared several things he had learned. 1) There isn't enough value put on networking and what you can learn from other people. This applies inside and outside of the organization. It is important to say yes to opportunities as many times as you can. You never know what doors will open. 2) There are a lot of people focused on short-term results. They come and go. 3) Most of us are working with a toolbox we developed over a series of jobs that may or may not be useful. In today's world our toolboxes are probably outdated so we have to stay open and learn. 4) Change starts from the top. If you don't have support at the top, you won't be successful.

The team at USA Fed threw out the old model and created a new one that allowed them to harness the power of their employees' creativity and dreams. The quote Rob ended our discussion with says it all. It's from Coach John Wooden. "It is what we learn after we know it all that counts." Rob understands that what is within can more powerfully change an organization than anything on the outside.

If we look about at our world, we see corporate greed of unimaginable proportions, collapsing and imploding institutions, and encounter an immense poverty of the spirit. We see endless war, warring politicians, and little reason to hope for a positive outcome. Newspaper headlines point to a justice system in question and retirement planning that has turned into survival planning. And, underneath it all is mounting hunger and illness, and a planet's distress that may just trump all other concerns.

The outside looks grim, but it is what's inside that matters. Five simple ways to prevent change are listed in *No Contest,* a gem of a book by Alfie Kohn.[23] His five ways offer insight into the task ahead of us. As I list each one, we might ask ourselves how familiar we are with them and see what's inside of us: 1) Limit your vision, 2) Adapt, 3) Think about yourself, 4) Be realistic, and 5) Rationalize.

Each one limits us. Each one makes something within want to scream in objection. Together they damn us and damn up our future potential. It is time to try something different, to create a new model that understands that unintended consequences and collateral damage are not acceptable casualties of life. When we set this understanding as our compass, something bigger holds our hands and hearts to the task, supporting us and steadfastly aligning us with the persons we were meant to be.

#6 — *Welcoming Unusual Answers and Solutions*

> *Once we rid ourselves of traditional thinking we can get on with creating the future.*
> — James Bertrand

Following the prior logic we free ourselves from the urge to turn back and the urge to turn our backs on each other. It is then that unusual answers and solutions begin to surface. At first these answers may seem crazy, unbelievable and impossible. They are not. Listening carefully we can gain a larger understanding. As we bring more minds and hearts into the process we access larger bits of information and see the next steps.

Sometimes, as if by magic, a plan will be laid out in its entirety. Other times, we are only able to see what is next, and believing in the plan may feel like stepping out into thin air. If we don't take the step, we won't be able to see the view from there, and will miss further insights that could change our businesses or our world. It feels like walking at the edge of a cliff. One misstep and it's a long fall, or with an evolutionary adjustment, it's one heck of an impressive flight.

It's all a matter of perspective. What do you think was going through Ben Franklin's head each time his experiments failed? Did he understand that his failures gave him access to a great deal more knowledge? Did he realize that with each sampling regardless of result, he knew more about what to do next? If he had stopped out of fear of failing, he would have never felt the exhilaration of success.

Each of us can be Ben Franklin as well as each organization. Life and business are both experimental. It's time to quit kidding ourselves and stop believing we know what we're doing. If Ben Franklin had *known* what he was doing, he might have been discouraged when what he thought he knew didn't prove true. All his tests packed with new knowledge and understanding might have been written off as experiments gone wrong. He would have missed the unusual answers and solutions, and we would have missed his great inventions.

One unusual answer is found in *The Art of Possibility*.[24] The Zanders call their remarkable practice *giving an A*. In Benjamin Zander's voice:

> "Yet, after twenty-five years of teaching, I still came up against the same obstacle. Class after class, the students would be in such a chronic state of anxiety over the measurement of their performance that they would be reluctant to take risks with their playing. One evening I settled down with Roz to see if we could think of something that would dispel their anticipation of failure. What would happen if one were to hand an A to every student from the start?"

Giving an A challenges every accepted belief about perform-ance reviews. Once initiated though, the Zander's experiment proved the wisdom inherent in their intuition. Starting from a belief in another's extraordinary capability has proven effective in scientific experiments in the school system, the military, and countless others. It is time for all workplaces to come on board.

When we see that it's all experimentation or it is yesterday's news, we turn possibility into probability, and invite the likelihood of industry-changing and world-defining ideas. In the process we lift an immense weight from the organization's shoulders, that once removed stimulates the workplace's instinctive creativity and natural inclination to innovate.

#7 — *The Quest After Limiting Beliefs and the Courage to Release Old Patterns*

Failure is only postponed success as long as courage coaches ambition. The habit of persistence is the habit of victory.

— Herbert Kaufman

As soon as new and unusual solutions begin to surface, more limiting beliefs are visible. We are capable of seeing our fears — the ways we protect ourselves — more clearly. This is useful. Even when it doesn't feel comfortable, it is important to remember that seeing these beliefs, and having the ability to consciously decide whether or not to believe in them, is much more powerful than having them dance about, just below the level of consciousness, silently and caustically running our programs.

When seen for what they are, these fears lose their punch. They are simply a fading echo of the past. A return to the first four logics at this time is helpful. The logics are not linear. They are interrelated and interdependent, like we each are on air to fill our lungs and a planet upon which to live, love, and grow.

As we turn and face the fear, we are gifted with the option of taking an initial step, however tentative, into *what is*. At the instant of seeing the belief we come face to face with the First Logic. We can choose to accept the fear or restricting thought as a part of *what is* or we can deny it. Of course, denial changes nothing. The belief persists and we slide back into the flaws of the past.

If we wisely choose acceptance of *what is,* we meet another point of choice. We can choose to further our adventure into the Second Logic of curiosity. The alternative is a serious-ity that steals our courage and sense of humor, necessary attributes for the quest.

Curiosity leads to the Third Logic and another choice. We can tighten up and revert back into seriousness and denial, although now knowing where that will take us, and slide a bit further into the hole we have dug for ourselves. Our openness to seeing this morsel of information differently, without old definitions and labels, will determine whether or not we have the sense to stop digging.

Before catching sight of the beliefs — mostly fear-based and limiting — we host these thoughts unconsciously, like a tapeworm stealing our nourishment. With new awareness, we have the choice to host the thoughts, not only consciously, but with gratitude for the additional insight they bring. Understanding grows as we uncover and bring more of our limiting beliefs out into the open.

Gary Kilmer knows about the power of courage when it comes to uncovering limited beliefs. He is the superintendent of the Oregon State Corrections Institution (OSCI), a men's medium security prison in Salem, Oregon. Gary took the reins of OSCI in February 2008. Not a traditional prison warden, Gary's long-term vision is to put himself out of a job. He recognized years ago that prisons weren't the answer, that as a society, we can't buy or build our way out of our problems. Prisons, in Gary's mind, define the failure of society. Early childhood interventions, addressing inequities, and making quality education available to all economic strata are at the top of his wish list. Plan A — lock people up, and Plan B — build more prisons to lock up more people, haven't worked. He says it is time for Plan C.

When I talk to the men inside they have noticed a marked difference since Gary came on board. While security and safety are still top considerations, the rigidity associated with that mindset has relaxed. Other things have changed too. Last year the inmates tended a one hundred foot by one hundred foot garden that produced six to eight thousand pounds of produce. The men saw the fruits of their labor. The experience was positive in many ways, not the least in the quality and freshness of the food. When people are involved rather than idle, everything is smoother. This year they expanded to three hundred feet by three hundred feet inside the walls and an additional two acres of potatoes outside the walls that are tended by men from a nearby minimum security facility. What potatoes they don't use they will share with other nearby prisons or give to the Oregon Food Bank. With an annual food budget of $804,000, Gary's gardens will help him cut the budget in thoughtful and productive ways.

The staff was skeptical at first. The idea of giving inmates access to tools could have been a stumbling block, so they built the program in partnership with the security team. When you are willing to take incremental steps you allow ideas, like plants, to grow. It takes hard work to stretch the corners on the boxes that over time, we have placed around the ways we do things. But, with courage and patience you can help people see that new is not dangerous and that stretching the back gardening, stretches us to new levels of trust and cooperation.

I asked Gary which values had been most important to him. The first one came pretty easily, value the ideas of others. Secondly, always listen. The third seemed to epitomize Gary's style, always ask why. He said, "That's where you'll find opportunity. People are hunkering down and waiting to see what to do next. In times of great uncertainty it is important to keep the staff engaged and live today even if tomorrow the last shoe drops. You still have choices as long as you are alive. When I get up in the morning I ask myself two questions, what am I going to do today and how am I going to do it better?"

Gary has the courage to believe in a better world. He knows that the world doesn't have to be the way it is right now. It can change. He ended with a quote from *Butch Cassidy and the Sundance Kid*.

Sundance: You just keep thinkin', Butch. That's what you're good at.

Butch: Boy, I got vision, and the rest of the world wears bifocals.

Gary's vision replaces limited beliefs. He sees value and opportunity when others see chaos and disaster. He looks at the world and finds ways to do things rather than reasons why he can't. And, he knows the road to wellness is paved one step at a time, with faith in a brighter future.

Buoyed by courage we too can fully engage the quest for limiting beliefs because we know it makes good common sense. As we enter into the spirit of experimentation, with no right or wrong results expected, we integrate the quest into our workplace and personal lives. The choice becomes choice-less and it then is only natural to keep our eyes open for every one of our limiting beliefs; they restrict our potential. The downside of refusing the quest need not be reiterated. The upside, the potential of personal and organizational fearlessness, is worth pondering and acting upon.

#8 — *Movement from me to the ME we were meant to be*

Life is no brief candle to me. It is sort of a splendid torch which I have got hold of for a moment, and I want to make it burn as brightly as possible before handing it on to future generations.

— George Bernard Shaw

Being a constantly evolving organization gives rise to an indisputable momentum that allows us to pass our legacies on to future generations. What legacy will we choose? Will our children's children look back upon the early 21st century and wonder what in the world we were thinking? Or, will our grandchildren smile, knowing we finally turned towards each other, and rewrote our stories of pain and suffering, of me versus you?

It is a story being written right now. The evolutionary shift is taking place. People are already choosing a *we* that includes *me,* knowing there is no survival for the *me* without the we. As we tread amidst the Eight Logics we are moving from separation into unity. Each logic is focused on bringing us together, and showing us the truth that we cannot evolve from a space of isolation and separation. We move forward only as we move forward together.

We hold a splendid torch in our hands and a sacred responsibility to our organizations, our families, and to generations as yet unborn. We each hold many clues to an intriguing riddle. Our clues are critical to a bigger truth. Not one of us is disposable. Each one of us leaves a hole when we hold back. We truly do require the marked presence of each other. We need each other in order to be whole again. We each, individually and collectively, are being called to move beyond self-concern, to concern for each other. By its very nature, we cannot do that alone. The time for separation has come and is now gone. We are learning the required lessons of an evolving society, and growing into more humane human beings.

If the auto makers from Detroit had infused their culture with curiosity, they would nonetheless have run into trouble, as Toyota found for itself in late 2008, since organizations tend to be insulated. But, if the automobile industry and people in workplaces around the globe had expanded our curiosity to include the world, its markets, and the overall ramifications of short-sighted decisions, we all could have moved from curiosity into innovative action. Together we would have seen the patterns forming on the horizon, and sought broader solutions across business, government and our communities to encompass and sustain the whole. Perhaps then, we would have chosen a different relationship with money, reevaluated our credit practices or developed conscious buying habits. Maybe the guy off the street would have had the money or been able to access the credit to purchase vehicles the auto makers manufactured. Common sense would have told us that a product was no good without a consumer capable of purchasing it.

When we move beyond *me* and instead choose the fullest expression that we each were meant to be, decisions cannot be made as irresponsibly. We learn from our mistakes, and see that acting in socially conscious ways is in our own best interest too. If we learned nothing more from past economic and personal pain, let us hope we learned that our decisions and actions are absolutely interconnected. When gas prices rose, all costs rose, and monies for mortgages, cars and other basic needs, slipped away. People living too close to the precipice of nothing cannot adjust, and we all are closer than we like to think. When enough slips away, the entire system implodes. We do not act in a vacuum. We are each affected by each other. When we understand this truth, we choose again and create from integrity and wholeness.

Together the Eight Logics offer an alternative imbued with the possibility of harvesting the genuine potential of each one of us. This does not exist within the current economic, social and political models. No one of us is useless. No one of us is so lost as to be unworthy of being found. Our own potential grows as we embrace each person. We acknowledge our native genius as we cherish the participation and well-being of others.

Everyday Common Sense

1. *The Present — seeing what is here now* — Stop; breathe a few breaths and allow yourself to be with whatever shows up. Consider viewing this moment and all of its attendant characteristics as ripe with possibility. What are you aware of as you breathe in this moment?

2. *Curiosity to see every aspect and possibility* — From your present situation, are you willing to suspend assumptions or actions in order to completely inspect every aspect of what is right in front of you?

3. *Openness to new answers* — New answers are everywhere and seem to be found primarily when we aren't looking. Are you ready to see everything and everyone as information rich, even those things you normally dismiss?

4. *Allowing time for the bigger picture to emerge* — Patience is yours if you choose it. Are you courageous and informed enough to slow down? Can you see the logic that speeding through the moment does not allow the picture time to develop?

5. *Garnering sufficient self-trust to see it through* — Can you let go of the need for proof and hold the course regardless? Are you willing to trust yourself and others with whom you so brilliantly surround yourself?

6. *Welcoming unusual and unexpected solutions* — When unusual or unexpected solutions appear we easily disregard them. Will you show rare common sense and receive them?

7. *The quest to unleash full potential* — Are you willing to see your collective and individual beliefs? What old ways stand between you and conscious evolution?

8.   *From me to the ME we were meant to be* — What parts of individual or organizational ego prefer personal and collective bankruptcy? What can accelerate your personal and organizational shift from exclusion to inclusion? What language or process redefinitions might be helpful?

Chapter 11

Now Is the Time

*First say to yourself what you would be; and then do
what you have to do.*

— Epictetus

The Force of Change Is Upon Us

To evolve or not to evolve is not the question. Evolution is a
fact. It is happening with or without us. We can end up like other
extinct species or we can open our eyes to the changing conditions
and let what is happening inform our actions. If we open our eyes
to the truth of our own experience and our growing understanding,
the choice is obvious. We know there is a better way. We are each
divining rods, capable of determining truth from falsehood and old
habit from enlightened understanding. At a deep level we already
know what is good.

We have always known this truth. Each time we assaulted
another's worth or had our own assaulted, it hurt. A bit of light left
our eyes and our goodness seemed a little more distant. In the words
of Khaled Hosseini in *The Kite Runner,* "There is a way to be good
again." To be good is what we all want. Our fear that we are not
good keeps us awake at night. It takes away our passion and

separates us from each other. It is the source of our internal conflict, the basis of our stress-filled world.

We know what is required for our organizations to consciously evolve. It is easier to tap into our innate courage when we use ourselves — what is true for us — as our guide. Then our choice is not something from a book. Our choice honors our internal compass, and starts the process of retrieving misplaced self-trust.

Now is the time to take a revolutionary leap in human consciousness — to rewrite the rulebooks on what is possible — and to stand right in the middle of personal authenticity and *for the benefit of us all* community. From this new baseline, anything and everything, known and as yet unknown, is possible.

What will we see, when from the future, we look back at these next ten years? What will be written about how we furthered this evolutionary shift? Will it be a story of courage, a story of movement from self-importance to the importance of us all? What magnificent potential will we have unleashed in the workplaces of today and tomorrow?

In a very short time we can find ourselves within a grander dream, a dream that if we are honest with ourselves, will fulfill us and add heartfelt meaning and purpose to our lives. Humans are hard-wired for community so inclusive that it denies life's fruits to no one. In the ancient words of Cicero, "We were born to unite with our fellow men and to join in community with the human race." Wise men among us have known our mandate as humans for thousands of years. Our hearts have always known this truth. Conscious evolution will not be forestalled another thousand years. It will not be denied another ten. The force of change is upon us. Now is the time for us to consciously choose who we will be, and to move from choice into unified action.

A Vision for the Future

1. Looking back from ten years in the future, what would you like written about your part in consciously evolving your organization and your life?

2. What would failure look and feel like to you?

3. What would success look and feel like to you?

4. What dream would you like to realize for yourself? For your organization? For humanity?

5. What do you imagine it would feel like to step forward into thin air and trust in your purpose and our purpose together?

6. If you knew the support of the universe was behind you, what would you do differently? And, what would you begin today?

7. What is the risk to you of doing nothing? Is taking the risk more or less of a concern than not taking the risk?

8. Now is the time to decide who you will be and what you are willing to believe in. What choice will you make? What three steps are you committed to taking in the next month...and over the next year?

9. Who will you join with to help build on your vision of the future?

Appendix I

Seven Workplace Essentials

The seven workplace essentials are characteristics of an evolved workplace. Each one builds on the power generated by the others. Together they christen the organization's capacity to be fully sustainable, capable of making a priceless contribution to society.

ME Management

It is important for every employee to be self-aware, emotionally mature, and personally responsible. When individuals are aware of their beliefs, thoughts and fears they are less likely to be reactionary and self-protective because they are attentive to their natural tendencies and automatic responses, and have learned to stop and clear their old programming to allow new ideas and solution to emerge. ME Management is not only self-awareness it also translates into responsible self-in-action. It is a first generation step into self-less service to the team, the organization and ultimately to society.

Financial Viability

In order to be in business tomorrow, organizations must think in terms of long-term profitability, learn to be resilient regardless of market changes, and offer valued products and services that

111

constantly and positively evolve. Financially viable organizations look at more than short-term gain. A financially viable organization is self-aware in a much larger sense. They are aware of their recruitment reputation, the probability of retaining the best talent, and their specific vulnerabilities to the competition, economy, and environment. They understand there is a deeper meaning present in the shifting landscapes. They know their viability depends on understanding the BIG picture. The world is their sounding board. Their job is to openly listen, literally and intuitively. Everyone from front line employees, old and new customers, management both satisfied and malcontent, to competitors and vendors, holds information critical to continued viability. Financially viable companies know and respect this. They are fired-up with the knowledge that the world is a gold mine and their job is to relentlessly dig for the treasure.

Shared Leadership

Shared leadership fosters enlightened decision-making, manageable workloads, better delegation, and people playing to their strengths. When seen through the lens of greater possibility, shared leadership shifts everything. The first thing that shifts is the whole idea of *leader* and *follower.* When there are leaders within the organization, there must be followers. When there is shared leadership, everyone is both leader and follower. People can't sit on the sidelines and wait for orders regardless of their position. The plus for the organization is obvious. The plus for employees, once understood and trusted, is being valued and respected. It is a real reason to come to work in the morning and give 100 percent. The implementation challenge lies in prying loose the need for control from both the leaders and the followers. But, when the organizational vision *appeals to the best that is in man,* working together to achieve that goal is a shared experience worthy of excellence.

Engaged People

We all want the same things from our jobs — trust, value, and respect that endorses maximal contribution. There actually is a magic pill that harnesses passionate employee engagement. We want to do good work with good people for a good cause. We want our work to have meaning. We want it to give us a sense of belonging and community. We want to contribute fully. We are tired of protecting ourselves with every breath. We want to feel safe enough to open up, learn and grow.

Curiosity Continuum

Creating a playful and inquisitive culture that encourages bold questioning may just be the cure for the serious-ity sickness prevalent in many organizations today. In fact, many are so serious that they have all but lost their innocent curiosity — the source of great ideas — choosing instead to be seriously safe. Having fun at work isn't the norm although some organizations are stepping out of the rut to rediscover the curiosity continuum, leaving no stone left unturned in search for outlandish solutions. It is a great game to hunt for what is possible rather than sticking to the company line or playing within the company's box. They know curiosity may just reveal something critically important to their future.

Perpetual Innovation

Ideas are the indispensable beginning point, the offspring of a culture imbued with creativity. Taking ideas and turning them into reality is the definition of good business. Workplaces that continually turn good ideas into reality regularly reinvent themselves and their concepts about business in general. They have an entrepreneurial-mindset that fuels constant strategic action. When employees willingly and passionately contribute, an *anything-is-possible attitude* begins to permeate the organization. That attitude drives a true rarity — perpetual innovation.

Sustainable Community

Humans are hard-wired for community. If we can't find it at work, and we have a basic level of self-confidence, we often choose to leave in search of a place to belong. We don't leave organizations. We leave people. When we are connected to our fellow workers, we stay. Imagine a positive workplace where we communicate, connect, and achieve for the good of our organizations, our communities, and our planet. Such an environment is the natural outcome of the first six workplace essentials. Sustainable communities are those in which individuals are included, appreciated, wanted, and useful.

Appendix II

Books for Continuing Evolution

In alphabetical order

Change or Die, Alan Deutschman, Regan, an imprint of HarperCollins Publishers, NY, NY, 2007

Managing from the Heart, Hyler Bracey, Jack Rosenblum, Aubrey Sanford, & Roy Trueblood, Dell Publishing, New York, NY, 1990

No Contest, Alfie Kohn, Houghton Mifflin Company, NY, NY, 1986

Presence, Peter Senge, C. Otto Scharmer, Joseph Jaworski & Betty Sue Flowers, The Society for Organized Learning, Cambridge, MA, 2004

Sway, Ori Brafman & Rom Brafman, Penguin Books, New York, NY, 2008

The Art of Possibility, Rosamund Stone Zander & Benjamin Zander, Penguin Books, New York, NY, 2000

The Grand Experiment, an Expedition of Self Discovery, Madren Campbell, Gayle Gregory & Karen Johnson, Pure Possibility, Hood River, Oregon, 2006

The Starfish and the Spider, Ori Brafman & Rod A. Beckstrom, Penguin Books, New York, NY, 2006

Who Are They Anyway?, BJ Gallagher & Steve Ventura, Dearborn Trade Publishing, Chicago, Ill, 2004

Appendix III

Resources for Continuing Evolution

In alphabetical order

Blue Fire Project, www.bluefireproject.org

It has been described as *social work for the Earth change times, therapy for the soul, outrageous, high style shamanism.* Blue Fire Project Programs are a way to grow that is fun, soulful, natural, creative, passionate, and deeply personally relevant. They connect small self with big Self, the personal and the planetary, heart and mind, soul and body.

Inei-Re, www.inei-re.org

The purpose of INEI-RE is to assist all who seek transcendence. This extraordinary and powerful ascension practice provides the keys to solve the riddle of existence. It is the path through the many veils of partial truth. This is the path of advaita (non-dualism), which embraces the holy in all traditions.

Pure Possibility, www.pure-possibility.org

Pure Possibility is home to The Fearlessness Project, a coaching and mentoring program that works with individuals, organizations, and within the Oregon State Corrections system to overcome limitation and embrace their true nature.

The Service Connection, www.theserviceconnection.org

The Service Connection brings women together in collaborative service to embody the skills needed to create a more sustainable future. Their programs are integrative shared leadership experiences focused on solving real world issues through an experience of unity that accesses the power of circle, transformative philanthropy, and a new paradigm for sustained giving.

Workplace Evolution, www.WorkplaceEvolution.com

Workplace Evolution (WE) is a resource bank of leading edge organizational development consultants. Their mission is to catalyze potential and nurture innovative workplaces to position organizations for success in our swiftly changing world. WE provides integrated solutions that benefit the organization, its individuals, and society as a whole.

End Notes

Chapter 1

1. Karen Youso, Change: Approaching Singularity, Minneapolis Star Tribune, February 2009

2. Rick Newman, 10 Cars That Sank Detroit, Flow Chart, USNew.com, April 2009

3. John P. Huchra, The Hubble Constant, Harvard, 2008

4. Ferdinand Pecora, Wall Street Under Oath: The Story of Our Modern Money Changers, Simon and Schuster, 1939

5. Lindsay Chappell, Toyota forgoes layoffs despite plant closings, Financial Week, Sept. 08, 2008

6. Peter Block, Transformation and the Structure of Belonging, Linkage – Best of Organizational Development Summit, May 2008

Chapter 2

7. Alan Deutschman, Change or Die, Fast Company, May 2005

Chapter 3

8. Aberdeen Group, All Aboard, Effective Onboarding Techniques and Strategies, January 2008

9. William G. Bliss, Cost of Employee Turnover, The Advisor

Chapter 4

10. Franklin D. Roosevelt, Inaugural Address, March 4, 1933, as published in Samuel Rosenman, ed., The Public Papers of Franklin D. Roosevelt, Volume Two: The Year of Crisis, 1933, New York: Random House, 1938

11. Campbell, Gregory and Johnson, The Grand Experiment, an Expedition of Self Discovery, Pure Possibility, LLC, Hood River, OR, 2006

Chapter 5

12. Herman Trend Alert, The pitiful State of Employee Engagement, August 2008

13. Gallup's List of Widely Admired People, Top 10, Final survey of the 20th century, 1999

14. Jennifer Levitz, Workplace Retirement Plans Suffer $2Trillion in Losses, Wall Street Journal, October 8, 2008

Chapter 6

15. A McKinsey Global Survey, Assessing the impact of societal issues, 2007

Chapter 7

16. Lawrence Pintak, Balancing Business with Buddha, June 2001

17. Lawrence Pintak, Jon Kabat-Zinn: The Prescription is Meditation, Shambhala Sun, September 1999

Chapter 8

18. Campbell, Gregory and Johnson, The Grand Experiment, an Expedition of Self Discovery, Pure Possibility, LLC, Hood River, OR, 2006

19. Susan Spencer, Make No Mistake, To ERR is Human, CBS Sunday Morning, March 22, 2009

Chapter 10

20. European Agency for Safety and Health at Work, Research on work-related stress, 2000

21. Alan Deutschman, Change or Die, Regan, an imprint of HarperCollins Publishers, NY, NY, 2007

22. Al Lee and Don Campbell, Perfect Breathing, Sterling, New York, NY, 2009

23. Alfie Kohn, No Contest, The Case Against Competition (Why we lose in our race to win), Houghton Mifflin Company, NY, NY, 1986

24. Rosamund Stone Zander and Benjamin Zander, The Art of Possibility, Penguin Group, NY, NY, 2002

About the Author

Gayle Gregory left behind a successful corporate career in 1997, unfulfilled and filled with the desire to find the missing pieces. With her husband, she crossed the Columbia Bar and turned left, headed for Mexico aboard her forty-foot sailboat. While there she was blessed with a moment that she calls grace. It provided the insights that became the groundwork for her understanding of fear and limitation, and what it takes to move through them into our natural, unrestricted potential.

After her return stateside, Gayle co-authored *The Grand Experiment, an Expedition of Self-Discovery* and founded Pure Possibility, the home of The Fearlessness Project, a coaching and mentoring program that works with individuals, and within the Oregon State Corrections system. She is a former senior manager with two Fortune 500 companies. In hindsight, both organizations prepared her well to champion conscious evolution.

Most recently she co-founded Workplace Evolution (WE), a resource bank of leading edge consultants whose mission is to catalyze organizational potential and nurture innovative workplaces. WE provides integrated solutions that benefit the organization, its individuals, and society as a whole. Gayle specializes in the deconstruction phase of WE's unique three-phase consulting process. As she says, "You can't build anew until you've dismantled the old foundation. It is the key. The foundation determines everything that comes after." Gayle is a veteran of radio talk shows, an inspirational coach, and a *take-no-prisoners* speaker. Her passion for personal and workplace transformation is unmistakable in every aspect of her work.

For more information please contact:

Workplace Evolution

http://www.WorkplaceEvolution.com

Gayle@WorkplaceEvolution.com